THE WORLD'S MOST AMAZING

HISTORY

FACTS

For Kids

THE WORLD'S MOST AMAZING
HISTORY
FACTS
For Kids

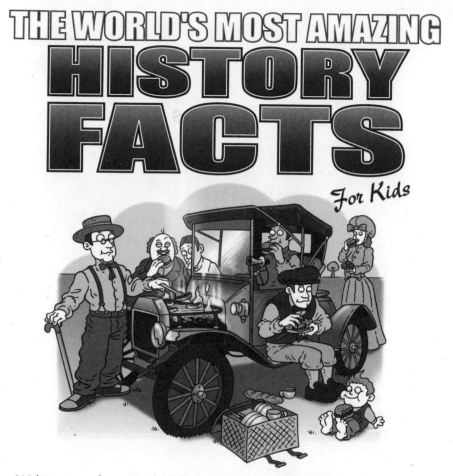

Written and compiled by Guy Campbell & Mark Devins
Illustrated by Paul Moran

GALWAY COUNTY LIBRARIES

EGMONT

We bring stories to life

First published in Great Britain 2003 as three separate books
(*The World's Amazing Crime Facts for Kids*, *The World's Most Amazing Battle Facts for Kids* and *The World's Most Amazing Inventions Facts for Kids*) by Egmont Books Limited.

This edition published in Great Britain in 2004 by Dean,
an imprint of Egmont Books Limited
239 Kensington High Street
London
W8 6SA

ISBN 0603 56152 7

Printed and bound in the U.A.E

10 9 8 7 6 5 4 3 2 1

CONTENTS

PART 1

BATTLE FACTS

CONTENTS

PART 2

CRIME FACTS

PART 3

PART 1
BATTLE FACTS

WACKY WARRIORS
Unusual Military Personnel

The costumes for the military series of Barbie dolls (Army, Air Force, Navy and Marine Corps) were approved by the Pentagon.

The German Kaiser, Wilhelm II, had a withered arm and often hid the fact by posing with his hand resting on a sword, or by holding gloves.

The Russian Navy's Dolphin Division, part of the old Soviet Black Sea Fleet, once had over a hundred dolphins in training. They were taught to jump, parachute from helicopters, locate underwater mines and lost equipment, and even to assassinate enemy divers and sink vessels.

US Civil War General Stonewall Jackson walked around with his right hand in the air because he thought it balanced the blood flow in his body. (He thought that his right hand was getting more blood than his left because he was right-handed.) Also, he never ate food that tasted good, because he assumed that anything that tasted good was unhealthy.

At an extravagant party during the reign of William III, the Honorable Edward Russell, Captain General of the English forces, used the fountain in his garden as a giant punch bowl for mixing drinks. The recipe included 2,550 litres (560 gallons) of brandy, 600 kilograms (1,300 pounds) of sugar, 25,000 lemons, 90 litres (20 gallons) of lime juice, and two kilograms (five pounds) of nutmeg. Russell's bartender rowed about in a small boat, filling up the punch cups for the awed guests.

A Mexican president once held a funeral for his own leg. The President, Antonio de Santa Anna, was the general who led Mexican troops to victory over Texan rebels at the siege of the Alamo in 1836. Santa Anna's leg was amputated below the knee after he was wounded during a battle with French troops in December 1838. He kept the leg at his hacienda near Veracruz for four years, during which time he rose to become dictator of Mexico and hugely popular with his people. On September 26, 1842, his supporters solemnly paraded the leg through the streets of Mexico City to the accompaniment of bands and orchestras, then laid it to rest in a national shrine known as the Pantheon of Saint Paula. Two years later, however, the leg was stolen during the riots that surrounded Santa Anna's fall from power. Santa Anna died in 1876 at the age of 62 – poor, blind and ignored. The fate of his leg remains unknown.

At the end of the Spanish-American War, in 1898, the United States occupied Cuba. Rioting mobs in the street, along with outbreaks of malaria and yellow fever, created havoc in the country. Lieutenant James Moss was sent with his troops to maintain order, which they did. The unique thing about Moss's 25th Infantry of only 100 men was that they were a bicycle corps – they all rode bicycles, they were all African-American, and they never once used their weapons the whole time they were in Cuba.

During the US Civil War, General Ulysses S. Grant believed that onions would prevent dysentery and other physical ailments. He reportedly sent the following message via wire to the War Department: "I will not move my army without onions." Within a day, the US Government sent three trainloads of onions to the front.

The Mongol conqueror, Timur the Lame (1336–1405), played polo with the skulls of those he had killed in battle. Timur also left a record of his victories by erecting ten-metre- (30-foot-) high pyramids made of the severed heads of his victims.

Poet and spooky writer Edgar Allan Poe was expelled from West Point, the United States military academy, because he turned up for a parade in his birthday suit. Poe appeared on a list of cadets who had committed most offences at the academy. In January 1831 he had 66 offences on his chart. The second most offending student on the list had just 21. He was ranked 74th best out of 86 students.

In World War One, a pit bull terrier named Stubby was awarded two medals – one for warning troops of a gas attack, the other for holding a German spy until American troops arrived. He also earned the rank of sergeant.

A TO Z OF FIGHTERS

Some Special Forces

Amazons

The Amazon River and Amazon jungle of South America were so named because tribes of female warriors were thought to live along the riverbanks. "Amazons" are tall, strong and fierce female warriors of mythology. They supposedly disfigured their bodies, removing one breast to perfect their skills with bows and arrows.

Conquistadors

Spanish soldiers who conquered the people of Mexico and Peru in the 1500s were known as conquistadors. In their search for gold, they enslaved the native people.

Cossacks

These amazingly skilled cavalrymen and soldiers from the southern part of Russia fought for the Russian Empire in the 16th and 17th centuries in return for special privileges. They also fought the Bolsheviks during the Russian Revolution and served in World War Two.

Crusaders

Crusaders were Europeans who went to the Holy Land (parts of modern Israel, Jordan and Egypt) from the 11th to the 13th centuries to "recover" Christian holy places from the Muslims. For some it was an excuse to plunder. Among the the crusaders was Richard 1 of England, who was the absent king during the days of the legendary Robin Hood. During the Children's Crusade in 1212, thousands of European children were sent to Egypt to fight. Many were sold into slavery; most died of starvation and disease.

Foreign Legion

In 1831, King Louis-Philippe of France formed the French Foreign Legion in order to keep his colonies under control. The Legion was made up of mercenary (paid) soldiers from different countries, and fought in both World Wars One and Two. Today there are about 8,000 soldiers in the Legion throughout the world.

Gladiators

Gladiators were trained fighters in ancient Rome. They fought each other, usually to the death, for public entertainment.

Guerrillas

Soldiers who ambush and sabotage their enemies – rather than fighting open battles – are called guerrillas. These tactics were used in the American Revolution, though the word "guerrilla" wasn't coined until 1809 during the Napoleonic Peninsula Wars.

Kamikazes
Japanese kamikaze pilots crashed planes into enemy aircraft carriers at sea during World War Two. Some 1,200 kamikaze pilots died sinking 34 American ships.

Rough Riders
During the Spanish-American War, a voluntary cavalry regiment from the US became known as the Rough Riders. (A rough rider is someone who can ride an untrained horse.) This regiment was made up of cowboys, miners and policemen, as well as upper-class horsemen.

Samurai
From 1100 to 1800, the Samurai (Japanese for "those who serve") were the warriors working for the aristocracy of Japan. Expert martial artists, they wore two swords as a sign of distinction.

Swiss Guard

This mercenary group was formed in the 15th century to guard the Pope. The Swiss Guard continues this function today in the Vatican City, the independent state within the city of Rome, Italy, where the Pope lives.

Vandals

The Vandals were a Germanic tribe. In the 5th century, they invaded the Roman Empire and attacked Rome. Today, the word "vandal" refers to someone who destroys things without reason.

Vikings

From the 8th to the 11th century, Viking warriors from Scandinavia raided and plundered the coasts of Europe. They also explored in their sturdy ships, travelling as far as Greenland and Newfoundland. The Vikings' favourite weapons were catapaults and battering rams.

WHERE THERE'S A WILL

William the Conqueror

William was born in 1027, son of the Duke of Normandy. The English throne was promised to him by Edward the Confessor, his cousin, but Edward changed his mind on his deathbed and passed the throne to Harold, Duke of Wessex.

William, enraged, invaded England. On October 14, 1066, he led the Normans to defeat the English under Harold II at the Battle of Hastings. At the height of the battle, the Normans retreated as if in defeat. Harold's armies broke ranks to pursue the beaten troops, only for William's army to turn on the ragged English force. Harold died in battle from an arrow to the head.

On Christmas Day, 1066, William was crowned King in Westminster Abbey, and reigned for 20 years.

In 1087, William led a battle against a French garrison at the town of Mantes. He won, but his horse shied away from a fiery ember and threw him into his saddle's iron pommel, bursting his intestines. He was carried to Rouen where he suffered a lingering death. His servants fled, leaving his swollen, dead body on the floor. It was rescued by a passing knight and a funeral was arranged. But the corpse was so bloated that, when it was squeezed into a stone tomb at the church, it exploded, and mourners ran out in horror.

William's son, William II, succeeded him and the British royal family has carried Norman blood from 1066 right up to the present day.

ARMY RATIONS

Some Tasty Military Inventions

During World War Two, American breweries that wanted to supply beer to troops abroad had to make them in special camouflaged cans. These khaki brews are highly collectable today.

In 1912, the first cannery opened in England. It was to supply food to the Royal Navy.

The first drive-through restaurant was a McDonald's in Sierra Vista, Arizona, a US military base. It was put in so the soldiers from Fort Huachuca could get food, since the base had a regulation prohibiting anyone in uniform from entering a business establishment.

K rations, named after A. B. Keyes, an American physiobiologist, were carried by Americans in World War Two. These lightweight packages included biscuits, canned meat, instant coffee, fruit bars, chewing gum, and powdered lemon juice. Sugar tablets and cigarettes were also included.

Since World War Two, American soldiers have been issued chewing gum with their K rations and survival kits. During World War Two, gum, considered an emergency ration, was also given to soldiers to relieve tension and dry throats on long marches. Soldiers used chewed gum to patch jeep tyres, gas tanks, life rafts, and parts of planes.

Part of an ancient Roman soldier's wages was paid in salt, valuable at the time. That's where we got the phrase "to be worth one's salt", and the word "salary".

US soldiers out in the field today are issued with MREs in case of emergency. MREs (Meals Ready to Eat) are brown plastic pouches that contain prepared meals, such as barbecued meatballs or corned beef hash, and are designed to last three years before spoiling.

"An army marches on its stomach."
So said Napoleon Bonaparte, aware that an army that eats well is likely to fight well. Military minds have often pondered the problems of feeding a moving army ...

Instant noodle soup and freeze-dried coffee were both military creations.

The "TV dinner" was introduced during World War Two because cans and metals were rationed during the War. The complete meals on a plastic tray proved to be a hit with American couch potatoes.

In 1918, food company Welch's developed a grape marmalade called "Grapelade". The first batch was purchased in its entirety by the US Army. It was an immediate hit with the military lower ranks, and became heavily in demand by ex-soldiers when they returned to civilian life.

Hippolyte Mege-Mouries developed margarine in France in 1869. Emperor Napoleon III had offered a prize for a suitable substitute for butter, for use by the French Navy.

On 25 October 1832, President Andrew Jackson signed an Executive Order dictating that coffee and sugar were to be substituted for the allowance of rum, whisky or brandy. From that day, coffee has remained a vital component of the US Army soldier's field ration.

Because of its use as a staple of American Navy messes since the mid-19th century, the humble white bean was christened the "navy bean".

In Malaysia in the 1960s, Australian soldiers working alongside British troops were paid an extra allowance because the food in the British Army ration packs was considered to be so poor. The Australian ration packs were bigger and tastier.

Charles Goodnight invented the first "chuck wagon", which he devised from an army wagon in the 1850s or 1860s. It was fitted with various shelves and compartments for storing food, cooking equipment, eating utensils, etc. It also had room for medical supplies, scissors and a shovel, because the cook's duties included acting as doctor and barber, and burying the dead.

In the 7th century, Welsh warriors were engaged in regular fighting with Saxons. The Welsh would each wear a leek on the battlefield to identify them. The leek thus became the national emblem of Wales.

Napoleon Bonaparte offered a prize in 1795 for a practical way of preserving food for his armies. The prize was won by a French inventor, Nicholas Appert, who devised airtight metal tins. It was the beginning of the canned food industry of today.

Captain Cook lost 41 of his 98-man crew to scurvy (a medical condition brought on by a lack of vitamin C) on his first voyage to the South Pacific in 1768. By 1795, lemons or limes were issued on all British Navy ships. British sailors became known as "Limeys" by their American counterparts.

Pies were a staple, portable ration of Roman centurions. Cooked meat wrapped in a basic pastry kept warm on long marches.

Christopher Ludwick, a German immigrant to Philadelphia, USA, made the city's first gingerbread. American Congress made him "Baker General of the Continental Army".

After winning the Battle of Hastings in 1066, William the Conqueror distributed English estates to his Norman friends. The French language started to work its way into English – *boeuf*, *mouton*, *veau* and *porc* are French words from which the English got beef, mutton, veal and pork.

Fish and chips was one of the few meals not to be rationed in Britain during World War Two. The forces ate them for energy, and fish-and-chip vans were laid on to take meals out to Londoners evacuated to rural areas.

RUN, IT'S THE ROMANS!

How the Legions Won the World

The Roman Empire was built largely on superior military strength and battle tactics. Here's how the Romans worked: Each soldier was extremely well trained, knew his battle plan, and was armed with a *gladius* (sword), two *pila* (javelins) and a *scuta* (shield).When meeting an enemy in battle, the footsoldiers marched forwards in a line with shields raised. At each flank would be the *ausilia* (auxiliary troops), protecting the footsoldiers from any attacks from the side. Behind these two units would be the cavalry, soldiers on horseback with longer swords ready to join the action once the infantry had finished its job.

The Romans would position themselves at the top of a rise, forcing the enemy to run up the slope towards them. When they were about 30 metres (90 feet) apart, a trumpet would sound in the Roman ranks, signalling the legionaries to throw their two javelins in quick succession.

The sight of several thousand javelins in the air at one time was terrifying to the enemy fighters, causing them to stop and crouch with their shields above their heads. This would be difficult as their own ranks further back would still be pushing forward, causing a crush of bodies. When the javelins landed, the points would pierce the shields and the shaft would fold under the impact, rendering the shields a useless tangle of wood and metal. The enemy had little choice but to throw down their shields and attempt to battle without them, among a hedge of tangled, broken javelins.

The Romans would then close ranks, each soldier holding his shield in front, charging the enemy in a wedge-shaped formation.

When the two armies met, the legion soldiers would thrust their shields forward into the enemy, causing injury and throwing the enemy soldiers off balance. Moving the shields to one side, the Roman soldiers would thrust their swords into their opponents. The swords would be withdrawn and shields brought forward ready for the next victim. The cavalry advanced after the legionaries had done their work, slashing down at the enemy from horseback.

The Romans didn't allow anyone to escape to fight another day. They believed in total victory, destroying the enemy's fighting power completely and permanently.

ALL AT SEA

Naval Nuggets

The first submarine attack took place in New York Harbour on September 6, 1776. The US sub, known as the *Turtle*, targeted the HMS *Eagle*, flagship of the British fleet, but became entangled in its rudder before it could lay any explosives.

During World War Two, a German submarine was sunk by a truck. The U-boat in question attacked a convoy in the Atlantic and then surfaced to see the effect. The merchant ship it sank had cargo strapped to its decks, including a fleet of trucks, one of which was thrown in the air by the explosion, landing on the sub and sinking it.

Baseball star, Yogi Berra, who was a catcher for the New York Yankees from 1946–1963, was enlisted in the US Navy during World War Two and participated in the D-Day landing on Omaha Beach on June 6, 1944.

"International Orange" is the official name of the paint used to paint the Golden Gate Bridge in San Francisco. Orange was chosen because it blended well with the span's natural setting. Had the US Navy's request been granted, the bridge would have been painted black with yellow stripes to aid shipping.

During World War Two, the US Navy commissioned the world's first floating ice-cream parlour for service in the Pacific. This concrete barge was capable of producing ten gallons of ice cream every seven seconds.

The naval phrase "splice the mainbrace" started out as a secret code. Naval officers in Nelson's time would have to supervise a ship in dry dock when it was in for maintenance. With not much to do, they would sometimes sneak off for a few shots of rum, telling the shipworkers they had to "splice the main brace".

The piratical exclamation "shiver me timbers" comes from an Old English reference to the masts of a ship. When the wind blows hard, the masts and sails begin to vibrate, shaking the entire ship and the sailors on board.

The front part of a ship or boat is called the "bow". This comes from the Old English word "bough", a strong branch on a tree. A master carpenter building a ship would find a tall tree with a large branch curving away from the trunk at a 45-degree angle. The trunk and bough would form the keel and bow of the ship.

On November 29, 1941, the programme for the annual US Army-Navy football game carried a picture of the battleship *Arizona*, captioned: "It is significant that despite the claims of air enthusiasts, no battleship has yet been sunk by bombs." Japanese dive bombers sunk the *Arizona* at Pearl Harbor nine days later.

In 1988, a bookseller from Cirencester, England, paid £5,575 for a lock of hair belonging to Vice Admiral Lord Nelson (1758–1805) at an auction.

In 1969 the US Navy spent $375,000 on an "aerodynamic analysis of the self-suspended flare". The study's conclusion was that the Frisbee was not feasible as military hardware.

MIGHTY MILITARIANS

Some Facts about the Battle Greats

The only member of General Custer's brigade to survive the battle at Little Bighorn was a Native American scout named Curley.

When US Civil War General Robert E. Lee took possession of the town of Chambersburg on his way to Gettysburg, the first thing he demanded for his army was 25 barrels of pickled cabbage.

Napoleon hit on the idea of using semaphore telegraph and gained a huge advantage over his enemies. He could send a message in flags from Paris to Rome in under four hours.

The "Red Baron", Manfred von Richtofen – Germany's air ace in World War One – was nicknamed by Allied pilots after his plane, a red Albatros fighter. The other pilots in his squadron also flew colourful aircraft, and the squadron became known as the "Flying Circus". Von Richtofen's 80-plus confirmed kills made him a feared and formidable opponent, a seemingly super-human pilot. But his luck ran out over France on April 21, 1918 when bullets from ground gunners and Canadian pilot Roy Brown ended his career and his life.

After leading the defeat of General Custer, Sioux Indian Chief Sitting Bull became an entertainer and toured the country with Buffalo Bill's Wild West Show.

In 1066, Halley's comet appeared shortly before William the Conqueror invaded England. The Norman King took it as a good omen; his battle cry became "A new star, a new king".

For more than 60 years in the 2nd century BC, the Carthaginians and the Romans fought for world power. For 16 of those years Hannibal, the Carthaginian leader, was able to hold off the Romans – until the battle of Zama. Though the Carthaginians had 15,000 fewer warriors, Hannibal thought he had the upper hand. He had 80 elephants, which he would use to send the Roman army fleeing in terror. Unfortunately, when Hannibal set the elephants free in the Roman ranks, the animals ran off in the opposite direction. Hannibal and his army lost the elephants, the battle, and the war.

Prime Minister Winston Churchill was born in a ladies' loo during a dance.

Parliamentarian and general, Oliver Cromwell, was hanged and decapitated two years after his death in 1658.

Alexander the Great had epilepsy.

Five members of Colonel Custer's family were killed at the Battle of Little Bighorn in 1876: Tom and Boston, two half-brothers; Harry Armstrong Reed, a nephew; and a brother-in-law, James Calhoun.

Julius Caesar was the first to employ coded communications, using what has become known as the "Caesar Cipher".

US President George Washington had to pay millions in protection money to pirates to stop them attacking US shipping, while Congress debated the creation of a US navy.

All of the officers in the Confederate Army during the US Civil War were given copies of *Les Miserables* by Victor Hugo to carry with them at all times. General Robert E. Lee, believed that the book symbolised their cause.

It was reported that Napoleon carried chocolate with him on his military campaigns and always ate it when he needed a boost of energy.

During the Napoleonic Wars, Napoleon's soldiers camped in the chapel of Santa Maria delle Grazie in Milan, where Leonardo da Vinci's famous painting of *The Last Supper* is located. The soldiers used the painting for target practice, which is why the face of Christ is almost obliterated.

Robert E. Lee, US Civil War leader of the Confederate Army, remains the only person to date to have graduated from West Point Military Academy without a single demerit.

Genghis Kahn's Mongol cavalrymen wore light leather armour made of horsehide hardened in animal urine.

Far from thinking him a bloody barbarian, modern Mongolians revere the name of Genghis Khan. His face appears everywhere, from bank notes to vodka labels.

JINGO LINGO

Some Weird War Words

A soldier wears a "havelock" on his head in the desert. It's a light cloth covering, attached to a military cap that protects the back of a soldier's neck from the sun. It was named after Sir Henry Havelock, a British officer serving in England.

In World War Two navy slang, an "airdale" was a naval aviation recruit.

Vikings would head fearlessly into battle often without armour, or even shirts. In fact, the term "berserk" means "bare shirt" in Norse, and the word came to describe their unhinged battling style.

The name "Jeep" came from the abbreviation used in the army for the "General Purpose" vehicle, G.P.10.

The word "tank" was used by the British as a code name for their new armoured vehicles in World War One. They wanted to preserve the element of surprise, and so they referred to the project by this innocuous name, which took hold and has lasted until today.

One explanation for the saying "it's so cold it could freeze the balls off a brass monkey" is that a brass monkey was a rack for storing cannonballs. When it got extremely cold, the monkey would freeze and become brittle, and the heavy balls would fall off.

"John has a long moustache" was the coded signal used by the French Resistance in World War Two to mobilise their forces once the Allies had landed on the Normandy beaches.

GOOD LORD!

Nelson at Trafalgar

In 1803, Admiral Lord Nelson was given command of the British fleet in the Mediterranean and blockaded the French fleet at Toulon for 22 months. When the French finally escaped, he pursued the fleet across the Atlantic to the West Indies and back to Spain, where it took refuge with the Spanish fleet in Cadiz. On October 21, 1805, the combined fleets ventured out of port, and found Nelson waiting for them off Cape Trafalgar. HMS *Victory*, Nelson's flagship, is the oldest commissioned warship in the world, and is still manned by Officers and Ratings of the Royal Navy. She is now the

flagship of Naval Home Command and lies in dry dock at Portsmouth Naval Base in England.

Detailed below are the main events of the Battle of Trafalgar, West of Cape Trafalgar, Spain, in 1805.

On Sunday 20 October a fleet of French ships was spotted by the British fleet sailing westward. Nelson, aboard the *Victory*, ordered the British fleet to form two columns.

The next day, in the early morning, *Victory* gave the order "Prepare for battle". By late morning, the French had begun firing on the British ship *Royal Sovereign*, which returned the fire. Before the real battle commenced, Nelson gave his famous rallying speech to the men aboard his fleet: "England expects that every man will do his duty".

Just before midday, the French opened fire on HMS *Victory*, shooting away the ship's wheel. *Victory*'s guns fired back into the rear of the French ship, *Buccentaure*.

At 1:15 in the afternoon, Admiral Lord Nelson was hit by a musket ball and taken below decks to be treated by the ship's doctor. He held on for a few hours, but died later that afternoon.

Despite Nelson's death and a fierce battle, the French were defeated at the Battle of Trafalgar. Lord Nelson became a great hero in England. His famous memorial is Nelson's Column, in Trafalgar Square in the centre of London.

RULES OF ENGAGEMENT

The Geneva Convention

The first international rules of war, known as the Geneva Convention, or Treaty, were made in Geneva, Switzerland, in 1864.

Rule 1: Warring nations cannot use chemical weapons.

Rule 2: The use of bullets or materials designed to cause unnecessary suffering is prohibited.

Rule 3: The discharge of bullets or rockets from balloons is prohibited.

Rule 4: Prisoners of war must be treated humanely and not used for propaganda purposes.

Rule 5: Prisoners of war must give their

name and rank or they will lose
their prisoner-of-war protection.

Rule 6: Nations must identify the dead and
wounded and inform families.

Rule 7: Killing anyone who has
surrendered is prohibited.

Rule 8: Hospital zones must be set up in
fighting areas for the wounded.

Rule 9: Protection from attack is granted to
hospitals showing the Red Cross.

Rule 10: The free passage of medical
supplies is allowed.

Rule 11: Shipwrecked armed forces at sea
should be taken ashore to safety.

Rule 12: Any army controlling another country
must provide food for the people.

Rule 13: Attacks on civilians and
undefended towns are prohibited.

Rule 14: Submarines cannot sink civilian ships
before passengers have been saved.

Rule 15: A prisoner can be visited by a
representative from his or her country.

DO YOU WANT A FIGHT?

Some Curious Conflicts

The shortest war on record was fought between Zanzibar and England in 1896. Zanzibar surrendered after 38 minutes.

Chevy Chase was a battle that took place on the English-Scottish border in 1388. It is now the name of a road in Los Angeles, USA, home to many Hollywood stars, and the name of an actual Hollywood star.

The Battle of the Herrings took place on February 12, 1429, at Rouvray, France, where French and Scottish troops attacked an English convoy taking salted fish to the English army attacking Orleans. The English repelled the attack.

In 1925, when the dog of a Greek soldier wandered across the border into Macedonia, the soldier ran after it and was shot by a Bulgarian guard. The Greek troops invaded Bulgaria in retaliation. More than 50 men were killed before the League of Nations intervened and stopped the war.

France and Mexico were involved in a year-long conflict known as the Pastry War in 1838. Mexico refused to pay for damage done by Mexican army officers to a restaurant run by a French pastry chef in Tacubaya, now a section of Mexico City.

In July 1969, tensions from a football match between the national teams of El Salvador and Honduras escalated into fighting. Salvadoran immigrants were then expelled from Honduras and the countries went to war. Some 2,000 people were killed in 16 days.

In 1325–37 a war was fought over a stolen bucket. When a group of soldiers from the city of Modena, in northern Italy, invaded nearby Bologna to steal a brown oak bucket, thousands of citizens were killed in the resulting fight. Bologna went to war with Modena to take back their bucket and restore their pride. The two cities fought for twelve years and thousands of lives were lost. Modena won the war, and the people of Bologna never got their bucket back.

In 1739, war was immediately declared after Captain Robert Jenkins appeared at the British Parliament, holding the remains of his ear in his hand. He claimed that the Spanish had cut it off after boarding his ship in the West Indies. The Spanish did not want English traders doing business in their American colonies and removed Jenkins' ear as a warning. The War of Jenkins' Ear went on for four years, with no clear winner.

WRATH OF KHAN

Genghis Khan – Ultimate Leader?

Genghis Khan was originally named Temujin when he was born around 1167. At the age of 13, he was fishing and caught a fish. His half-brother grabbed the fish for himself. Temujin immediately drew an arrow and shot his half-brother dead. As an adult, he proved a natural leader, uniting the nomadic tribes of Mongolia and becoming master of the new empire he had created. He was given the title Genghis Khan, which has been translated as "Greatest of Rulers", "Emperor of All Men", and "Ultimate Leader". His conquest of China began in 1215 and was ultimately completed by his grandson, Kublai Khan.

So awesome was the prospect of Kahn's army, that when Peking surrendered to the Mongols in 1215, 60,000 girls were so terrified of capture that they threw themselves from the city walls to their deaths.

Genghis Khan established a pony-express system that spanned his entire empire. And his battle tactics were often inspired. Legend has it that when he held an enemy city under siege, he demanded 1,000 cats and 10,000 swallows from the inhabitants. When these were delivered, he tied cloths to their tails and set them on fire. The animals fled home, setting fire to the city and allowing it to be taken.

Genghis's Mongol cavalry was unparalleled. Excellent horsemen, under Kahn they were an unstoppable fighting force. They had ingenious techniques that would make it appear that their numbers were larger than they really were: each horseman had multiple spare horses with him, mounted with dummies. As a result, historians disagree about the actual size of the army. Estimates range from a hundred thousand or so to close to a million soldiers.

Legend has it that Khan was buried in 1227 beneath a spreading tree in the mountains that he had chosen many years before. Forty horses were said to have been killed and buried alongside him for use in the afterlife. His soldiers also killed all witnesses to the funeral, including animals, and then killed themselves, so that no living being could possibly know the tomb's location. The story goes that saplings grew so thick around the grave that in time, that it became swallowed in an impenetrable forest, never to be seen again.

THE LITTLE GENERAL

Napoleon Meets his Waterloo

Napoleon was born on the island of Corsica one year after it became French property. As a boy, he hated the French.

Even so, he attended the Paris Military Academy and was in Paris during the French Revolution. When France became a Republic in 1792, he was promoted to Captain. After defeating the Italian armies in 1796 and the Austrians in 1797, he was made General. In November 1799, he overthrew the French Directory to become First Consul of the Government. Just twelve years after the monarchy was disposed of in the French Revolution, Napoleon changed France from a consulate to an empire, with himself as Emperor.

By 1812, Napoleon had wiped out the last traces of the Holy Roman Empire and conquered most of Europe. But after a disastrous battle against Russia, his enemies struck back.

On March 18, 1814, the Allies – Britain, Prussia, Austria and Russia – marched into Paris. Napoleon gave up the throne on April 6, 1814, and was sent into exile on Elba, a tiny island off the coast of Italy. The French monarchy was restored, but not for long. By popular demand, Napoleon returned to France on February 26, 1815 with a handful of troops and was returned to power within just 23 days.

The Allies united for a final campaign against him; a campaign which would decide the future of Europe. Napoleon decided to strike quickly, as to delay would allow the Allies time to muster vast forces. Crossing the border into Belgium on June 15, his plan

was to destroy Prussian and British armies there before the Austrian and Russian armies could arrive.

The Battlefield at Waterloo was only five kilometres (three miles) wide and two and a half kilometres (one and a half miles) deep. On it were massed over 140,000 soldiers.

The British Commander, the Duke of Wellington, chose his ground carefully. He deployed his troops behind a ridge to protect them from cannon fire but with woods behind for cover should things go badly. Wellington had been promised help from the Prussian General Blucher, and the arrival of these reinforcements late in the battle turned the tide. On such a small and muddy battlefield, there was no room for skilful manoeuvres, so the battle became a series of brutal frontal assaults by Napoleon's forces. The French had made

little progress, but the relentless assaults were starting to tell on the British troops. With Prussian help, a last attack by the French Imperial Guard was routed and panic started to spread through Napoleon's forces.

The Allies lost 55,000 men and French 60,000. Napoleon's last great gamble had failed and he was exiled to the island of St Helena in the South Atlantic, were he died six years later. Had he won, France could have ruled Europe for centuries to come.

The wallpaper in Napoleon's bedroom on St Helena was dyed with Scheele's Green, a pigment that contained copper arsenite. In 1893, an Italian biochemist called Gosio found that if wallpaper containing Scheele's Green became damp, the mould converted the copper arsenite into a poisonous, vaporous form of arsenic. It is possible that Napoleon's wallpaper was largely responsible for his death.

MY KINGDOM FOR A NORSE?

The Battle of Stamford Bridge

The Battle of Stamford Bridge in 1066 was one of the most important in English history. Firstly because it was the last Viking invasion and battle on English soil, and secondly because it forced Harold II's English army to march north to Yorkshire to meet the Vikings, allowing William the Conqueror to land his Norman army to the south without opposition.

The Viking force was lead by Norwegian King, Harald Hardrada, and Tostig, King Harold of England's own brother. In the early skirmishes, the Vikings kept their own battle order and the English forces could make little headway. But suddenly the

Vikings broke ranks and tried to drive the English from the field with a brutal man-to-man assault. The better organised English were then able to attack from all sides with arrows and spears, and during the assault, Hardrada, the Norwegian king, was struck fatally by an arrow in the neck. The Vikings retreated, and Tostig, Harold's brother, took up their banner.

Both armies re-organised and there was a long pause in the battle. Harold offered his brother peace, but the battered Vikings refused, preferring to die on the field than negotiate any kind of surrender with the enemy.

Tostig's army sent up a war cry and the battle began again. Viking reinforcements, led by Eystein Orri, arrived from their invasion ships. But Orri's men were exhausted by their hasty journey from the coast, and the English forces easily defeated them. When the slaughter was over, Harold was merciful to his (now dead) brother's defeated army, and the Viking survivors were allowed to go home in 24 ships. They had arrived in 300. But Harold had no time to rest. His troops now faced an even greater foe on the south coast of England. When Harold's remaining men arrived at Hastings – after a 650-kilometre (400-mile) forced march from Yorkshire – William the Conqueror's Norman invasion force had already landed and marched inland to take up good defensive positions, ready for Harold's arrival.

At Hastings, the course of English history changed. Without the ravages of Stamford Bridge, the English army may well have defeated William the Conqueror's Norman invasion force and, for better or worse, the shape of Europe – and consequently the world – would have been very different.

BY GEORGE!

America's Revolutionary Hero

On April 18, 1775, the British Army fired on the American militia in Boston. Battles ensued and, as word spread of the British assault, Americans from near and far assembled near Boston to fight.

The young George Washington took charge of this army on July 3. The new Commander found that his army was woefully under-armed, and had the British known this, they probably could have ended the Revolution before it had even started. However, they didn't know, and Washington managed to keep his enemy in ignorance. Indeed, the British fled Boston, leaving a supply of cannon, small arms and military stores to the value of £50,000, which was quickly taken by Washington's army.

The British regrouped and were joined by the British fleet, with between three and four hundred ships. Troops also arrived from the south, and soon 30,000 soldiers stood ready to annihilate the American army.

The British planned to seize New York and then the rest of the country, bringing the war to a speedy end. As they landed and established themselves in and around New York, Washington kept close watch. He had 9,000 men in a fortified camp at Brooklyn, and on August 22, he learned that the enemy had landed 10,000 men and 40 cannon at the lower end of Long Island. The battle there was a defeat for George, but British casualties were heavy. While the British licked their wounds, Washington quietly secured all available boats and, under cover of night and a dense fog, withdrew his forces. He retreated, leading the British to believe his threat was over.

Not so. In bitter ice and snowstorms, Washington's men marched on the British at Trenton, New Jersey, and took it. And, with a river between his forces and the British, he was able to hold it.

To stop his makeshift army from going back to their farms, Washington and his officers used their own private fortunes to pay their soldiers, keeping the army together. After two years, he had the British once again confined to New York. The frustrated British then attempted to take the South. The southern conflict ebbed and flowed until an exciting close of hostilities at Yorktown in 1781. Washington had kept his army of amateurs together, instilling in them his rules of engagement in battle:

1. Never attack an enemy position which is prepared or entrenched – always make surprise attacks.
2. Charges by cavalry should be made if possible on the flanks of infantry.
3. The first quality of a soldier is strength under fatigue and hunger.
4. Nothing is so important in war as an undivided command.
5. Never do what the enemy wants you to.
6. An ordinary general, in a bad position against superior force, seeks safety in retreat; but a great captain marches to meet the attack.

The end of the struggle for liberty came on October 19, 1781, with the British surrender at Yorktown. Britain acknowledged the independence of the United States and, in 1783, a treaty of peace was signed at Versailles in France. Washington became America's greatest son, and one of the most respected military leaders in world history.

BABANGAS R US

A World of Weapons

Babanga: African sword consisting of a metal leaf-shaped blade on a wooden hilt.

Baggoro club: Flat club from Australia made of hardwood with a sharpened edge.

Biliong: Malaysian axe consisting of a square blade fitted into a wooden handle.

Bokken: Wooden Japanese practice sword.

Bolas: Three-armed leather thong with stones at each end. The weapon is spun around the head and then thrown at the enemy's legs to bring him to ground. Popular in ancient South America.

Boomerang: Australian throwing stick with a range of about 20 metres (60 feet).

Burrong: Wooden club from Australia carved into an axe-like shape.

Campilan: Malaysian sword with a forked wooden end tied with tufts of dyed hair.

Chakram: An Indian flat steel ring with a sharpened outer edge used as a throwing missile; several were often carried on a pointed turban. It is thrown like a Frisbee.

Chijiriki: Japanese spear with a chain attached to the end; two-handed weapon.

Claymore: Two-handed sword popular among Scottish clan fighters between the 15th and 17th centuries. Measuring up to two metres (six feet) long, the handles were up to 60 centimetres (two feet) in length.

Craquemarte: Heavy European sword with a curved blade, generally used at sea.

Cumber-jung: Indian flail. Two heavy quoits attached to a short wooden handle by chains.

Dolabra: Axe-like Roman weapon with a socketed head attached to a wooden handle.

Fang: All-iron Chinese weapon with two double-edged blades at the end of a handle.

Flagellum: Three-pronged Roman whip.

Gargaz: Indian mace with six to ten blades on the head made of steel attached to a chain.

Gladius: Short Roman thrusting sword for legionaries in close battlefield combat.

Goddara: Turkish sword with a curved blade and padded hilt, often highly decorated.

Gunsen: Folding fan with iron sticks used by the Japanese as an attacking shield.

Kan sin ke: Chinese whipping chain made of short metal bars joined with links.

Kheten: Egyptian two-handed axe with a bronze head fitted into the wooden haft.

Kyoketsu-shogi: Japanese ninja weapon; a rope connects a metal ring and a forked knife. Also used to aid climbing.

Metsubishi: Japanese weapon designed to blind an enemy: a small, wooden box is hollowed out and filled with pepper or dust, and it is then used like a blowpipe.

Nagegama: Japanese chain weapon with a short blade attached to a handle by a long chain, thrown at attackers and then retrieved to use again.

Pacho: Wooden club from the South Pacific with shark-teeth edges.

Pagaya: Paddle-shaped club from Brazil.

Quaddara: Persian straight-bladed sword, often inlaid with gold and precious stones.

Tomahawk: Native American combat axe and pipe: the iron blade is fitted with a pipe bowl, the handle is hollow and forms the pipe stem.

Tschekan: Hefty Russian war hammer with a blunt steel head.

Tuagh-gatha: Scottish battle-axe.

Veecharoval: Indian scythe-type weapon with a curved, metal blade on a wooden handle.

Zagbnal: steel-beaked axe from India, often engraved and inlaid with gold.

BATTLE BITS

Miscellaneous Military Morsels

During the Battle of Gettysburg, Pennsylvania, in the US Civil War, the only civilian to die was 20-year-old Mary Virginia "Jennie" Wade, who was shot through the heart while making bread.

150 years ago, surgeons never washed their hands after an operation, because all blood was assumed to be the same.

Over 300 of the soldiers killed in the American Civil War were 13 years old or under, and 25 were under ten. Most of these casualties were fife players or drummers, but children regularly enrolled as combat troops.

During the Crimean War, from 1853 to 1856, the British Army lost ten times as many troops to dysentery than to injuries sustained on the field of battle.

In Japan, the dragonfly symbolises good luck, courage and manliness. Japanese warriors often wore the dragonfly emblem in battle.

Rebecca Elizabeth Marier was the first woman to graduate top of the class at West Point, the US military academy, based on her academic, military, and physical accomplishments.

During the 1940s, cosmetics company Revlon contributed directly to the war effort, by manufacturing first-aid kits for the US Navy.

The earliest known photograph of the US star-spangled banner was taken at the Boston Navy Yard in 1873.

Between 1861 and 1865, at least 618,000 Americans died fighting the Civil War.

3,530 Native Americans fought for the Union side in the American Civil War. 1,018 of them were killed in action.

In addition to those who died due to battle and disease, the Union side in the US Civil War listed sunstroke fatalities at 313.

During World War Two, the American automobile industry produced a grand total of 139 cars. Instead of making cars, the industry manufactured the tanks, planes, boats and bombs used by the Allies in the war. The Ford Motor Company alone made more military products than the whole of Italy during the war years.

Medieval battering rams, used to smash down castle gates, were covered in a frame of wet animal skins called "sows" or "cats".

Louis XIV of France, the Sun King, was obsessed with fashion. When his troops occupied the city of Strasbourg in 1681, he ordered its citizens to wear French style clothing within four months.

The ancient Roman armies made the first ever machine gun, a wooden contraption which could fling many bolts in rapid succession.

Sideburns, long growths of beard down the sides of a man's face, were originally named "burnsides" after US Civil War General Ambrose Everett Burnside, who wore them in the field and started a fashion for them among officers and troops.

A fletcher is a person who makes arrows.

When Chinese Qin Shi Huang died in 210 BC, 7,500 terracotta archers, soldiers, chariots and horses were buried with him in his tomb.

In the Middle Ages, a knight who led troops into battle was entitled to carry a banner. This banner, emblazoned with his colours or a family symbol, was useful for rallying troops in the confusion of battle. The form of the banner depended upon the rank of the knight and size of his army. Knights with small household units bore a small triangular pennant. Knights with larger groups (and therefore larger banners) were known as "knights banneret".

A quarrel was originally a bolt to be fired by a bow or crossbow.

The shaped top walls of a medieval castle, designed to protect the defenders against invasion, are called crenellations.

Confederate US Civil War General Robert E. Lee married a relative of George Washington, Mary Ann Randolph Custis. She owned a big house called Arlington, and they lived there for 30 years until Lee resigned his commission. The Lees left the property in 1861 and Union troops occupied it. 200 acres were set aside to bury fallen Union soldiers. Today over 250,000 war dead are buried there and it is known as Arlington National Cemetery. The cemetery is maintained by the US Army, but veterans of all military services are eligible to be buried there if they died on duty, are retired from the military, or have received the Medal of Honor, Distinguished Service Cross, Purple Heart, or Silver Star.

The present-day Vatican is the smallest sovereign state in the world. It has its own army – the Swiss Guard – and the right to have its own navy.

Spiral staircases in medieval castles go clockwise as you climb. This is because all knights used to be right-handed. An intruding army climbing the stairs would be less able to use their right hands to fight with swords because of the awkwardness of negotiating the staircase. Left-handed people would have had no problem, but they were banned from becoming knights, because left-handedness was thought at the time to be a sign of the Devil's descendants.

Medieval knights put shark skin on their sword handles to give them a more secure grip; the sharp scales would dig into their palms.

Armoured knights used to raise their visors to identify themselves when they rode past their king. This custom has evolved into the modern military salute.

If a statue of a military person on a horse has both front legs in the air, this indicates that the person died in battle; if the horse has one front leg in the air, it means the person died as a result of wounds received in battle; if the horse has all four legs on the ground, the person died of natural causes.

Playing cards were issued to British pilots in World War Two. If captured, they could be soaked in water and unfolded to reveal a map for escape.

The term "the whole nine yards" comes from World War Two fighter pilots in the Pacific. When arming their planes on the ground, the machine gun ammunition belts measured about eight metres, or nine yards. If the pilots fired all their ammo at a target, it got "the whole nine yards".

The colour khaki was first used by soldiers during the Afghan War in 1880.

Man's best friend has often been used as an ally in times of war. Ancient Romans and Gauls used dogs to fight on the field. In the 15th century, the Spanish sent dog warriors into battle that wore quilted overcoats as a protection from archers.

During World War One, cats lived with soldiers on the front line, where they killed the mice that ran wild in the trenches.

Before radio telephones were invented, carrier pigeons took messages between battleships at sea.

In 19th-century Europe, messenger pigeons were sent out two at a time because falcons were trained to attack them, thereby intercepting the message.

During World War Two, US scientists tried to train bats to drop bombs. They failed.

Attila the Hun died after getting a nosebleed on his wedding night.

The Battle of Agincourt in 1415 was part of the Hundred Years War between the French and the English, and an early example of superior arms triumphing over superior numbers of troops. The English army, led by Henry V, had marched across northern France through thick mud, and was massively outnumbered by the fresher French army. English archers, with their longbows, were able to keep the French, with their crossbows, too far away to shoot. The French decided to charge. The muddy ground caused problems for their heavily armoured troops. The French lost at least 5,000 men, including many of the greatest French aristocrats, and another 1,000 were captured. English losses totalled just 140. The victory helped establish Henry V as King of England, and brought him close to his dream of uniting the French and English thrones.

The nearest thing to a tank in ancient times was an elephant. Battle elephants were used by Hannibal of Carthage when he crossed the Alps to fight the Romans. Elephants with carriages on their backs were able to hold four soldiers at a time.

Alexander the Great conquered India with the help of elephants.

The Greek king Pyrrhus and his men rode elephants into battle against the Romans. Although the Greeks won, their losses were massive, and today the phrase "Pyrrhic victory" is used to mean any victory won at great cost.

In the 16th century, Emperor Akbar of India used elephants in battle. The elephants were hung with bells in order to sound frightening, and their trunks were bound to straighten them, with poisoned daggers attached to the ends.

The doors on US nuclear missile silos weigh 748 tons and take 19 seconds to open.

The Dickin Medal was introduced in Britain in 1943 to honour animals which made outstanding wartime contributions. It is the animal version of the Victoria Cross, awarded for service beyond the call of duty. The medal is named after Mrs M. E. Dickin, CBE – who founded the People's Dispensary for Sick Animals – and it was first awarded in 1943. The medal has been awarded to 59 animals in all, including 32 carrier pigeons, 19 dogs, three horses and a ship's cat.

An all-women squadron of bomber pilots, called the Night Witches, flew for the Soviet Union during World War Two. The squadron – the 588th Night Bomber Air Regiment – won 23 citations for "Hero of the Soviet Union", Russia's highest award for bravery.

The death of Major McCook in battle during the US Civil War completed a sad set of coincidences in his family history. His youngest son, Charles McCook, was killed at the Battle of Bull Run on July 21, 1861. His other son, Robert McCook, was killed on July 21, 1862. The Major himself was killed on July 21, 1863.

The American Civil War has long been known for its "firsts." These include the first hospital ships, Medals of Honor, cigarette and tobacco taxes, income tax and the first ever photographs of battle.

During the US Civil War, telegraph wires were strung to follow and report on the action on the battlefield. But there was no telegraph office in the White House, so President Lincoln had to go across the street to the War Department to get the news.

The Aztec Indians of Mexico believed turquoise would protect them from physical harm, and so warriors used these green and blue stones to decorate their battle shields.

Before all-porcelain false teeth were perfected in the mid-19th century, dentures were commonly made with teeth pulled from the mouths of dead soldiers following a battle. Teeth extracted from US Civil War soldier corpses were shipped by the barrelful to English dentists.

Jersey, in the Channel Islands, was the only part of Great Britain that the Nazis occupied during World War Two.

Soldiers arrived to fight the Battle of Marne in World War One not on foot or by military plane or military vehicle, but by taxi. France took over all the taxi cabs in Paris to get soldiers to the front.

The top ten ranks of the British Army are:

1. **Field Marshal**
2. **General**
3. **Lieutenant General**
4. **Major General**
5. **Brigadier**
6. **Colonel**
7. **Lieutenant Colonel**
8. **Major**
9. **Captain**
10. **Lieutenant**

Cannons were first introduced in the 1300s, but they were so unreliable that they often exploded when firing.

Betsy Ross's other contribution to the American Revolution, besides being credited with designing and making the first ever American flag, was that she ran a bomb factory in her basement.

Since Napoleon's crushing defeat by Wellington at the Battle of Waterloo, the word "Waterloo" has since come to mean a disastrous defeat of any nature.

The only two Southern state capitals not occupied by Northern troops during the American Civil War were Austin, Texas and Tallahasse, Florida.

Annual global spending on defence totals more than $700 billion. Global spending on education is less than $100 billion.

James Arness, the actor best known for playing Marshall Matt Dillon in the long-running TV series *Gunsmoke*, was the first US soldier to jump off his boat at Anzio in Italy in 1944. He was ordered to do so because he was two metres (six feet eight inches) tall and the water's depth needed to be tested as a safety precaution.

The first recorded revolution took place around 2,800 BC when people from the Sumerian city of Lagash overthrew bureaucrats who were stealing public money while raising taxes.

The longest conflict on record was the so-called Hundred Years War between Britain and France. It actually lasted 116 years, ending in 1453.

The very first bomb that the Allies dropped on Berlin in World War Two killed the only elephant in the Berlin Zoo.

The Japanese confiscated chess books during World War Two, thinking they were military codes. Japan did not have an organised chess federation until 1968.

The extras in the battle scenes in the movie *Braveheart* were reserves in the Irish army.

The US government estimated in 1863 that the Civil War was costing $2.5 million every day. An estimate in 1879 of the cost of the whole war totalled $6,190,000,000.

Confederate soliders in the US Civil War were often farm boys who didn't know left from right, but they knew hay from straw. To teach them to march, officers put a stalk of hay in one shoe and a stalk of straw in the other and shouted, "HAY FOOT! STRAW FOOT!" instead of "LEFT, RIGHT!"

In feudal Japan, the Imperial Army had special soldiers whose only duty was to count the number of severed enemy heads after a battle.

The space between government and opposition benches in the British Houses of Parliament was designed to be two and a half sword lengths wide to avoid incidents between armed members.

The walls of an igloo stand up better to modern artillery than concrete, according to tests conducted by the Swedish army. The walls absorb an artillery blast, are almost invisible from the air, and can't be spotted by the infra-red sensors that guide missiles.

During the American Revolution, more inhabitants of the American colonies fought for the British than for the Continental Army.

To pass US Army basic training, female recruits must do 17 push-ups in two minutes. Males must do 40 push-ups in two minutes.

During the Vietnam War, American soldiers used Slinky toys as radio antennae by stretching them between two trees.

Some Viking spearsmen could reportedly throw two spears at once using both hands, and even catch a spear in flight and hurl it back.

During World War Two, the Japanese Army could not break the "secret code" of the US Marines. The code was simply a group of Native American volunteers speaking their own Navajo language over the field radios.

Peter Karpin, a German spy in World War One, was seized by French Intelligence agents in 1914. Keeping his capture a secret, the French sent faked reports from Karpin to Germany and intercepted his wages for three years until he escaped in 1917. With those German funds, the French purchased a car which, in 1919 in occupied Germany, accidentally ran down and killed a man, who turned out to be Peter Karpin.

According to the Recruitment Code of the US Navy, anyone bearing an "obscene and indecent" tattoo will be rejected.

Mata Hari, who was executed by firing squad in France in October 1917, is probably the most famous spy of all time. Yet she was nothing of the kind. The evidence of her alleged espionage on behalf of the Germans is based on her being mistaken for a known German agent, Clara Benedix. It was only in 1963, when her secret files were released, that her innocence was revealed.

Long-handled Viking battle-axes were sometimes used instead of swords in open combat. As the owner could not hold a shield at the same time, he would take cover behind the front line of warriors, jumping out at the right moment to hack down the enemy.

Viking craftsmen often named the swords they made. Examples have been found called "Gold-hilt" and "Leg-biter".

The very first cannons fired heavy arrows, but soon stones were used as well. They were used on a large scale only after 1325. The English king, Edward III, employed them with great success at the siege of Calais in 1346.

A highly coveted item of clothing is the Battle of Britain tie, which was designed by, and is still sold at, Gieves and Hawkes outfitters in London. Only British airmen who fought in the battle are entitled to wear this dark blue tie, which bears the rose of England and a tiny outline of the British Isles woven on it in gold. The company will only sell one after receiving proof of identity.

The famous Viking warriors known as "berserks" would work themselves into a battle frenzy so intense they would bite their own shields. In battle, they could even ignore the pain of wounds and fight on regardless.

The name "Dixie" became a universal nickname for the American South long before the Civil War. The French heritage of Louisiana city was clearly shown on the ten-dollar bills produced by its banks, which had the word "Dix" (French for "ten") on the corner. To non-French-speaking tradesmen, these bills were known as "Dixies", and the great river basin of the lower South became "Dixieland."

George Washington was in command of the first US Navy created in 1775. It started with four ships. The ships were sold after the War of Independence and the "real" navy began in 1798.

During World War Two, the US Navy's world champion chess player, Reuben Fine, calculated where enemy submarines might surface, on the basis of positional probability.

During medieval times, soldiers sometimes threw dead animals, severed heads and the bodies of plague victims over the walls of besieged cities in an attempt to spread disease among the defenders.

World War Two Italian dictator Benito Mussolini was once expelled from school for knifing a fellow pupil.

In Ancient Sparta, seven-year-old boys were trained as soldiers. They were taught military skills, obedience and endurance of pain.

Agamemnon, the legendary king who led the combined Greek forces against Troy, sacrificed his own daughter Iphigenia to the goddess Artemis. He was later murdered in the bath by his wife.

Abbad el Motaddid, Moorish king of Spain, used his enemies' skulls as flowerpots.

The steward of a naval vessel looks after the welfare of the crew. The word comes from the Anglo-Saxon word "styweard", meaning a keeper of pigs.

The Battle of Marathon is famous, not only because the underdogs won, but also because of a legend of courage and sacrifice. Darius – the leader of Persia, Egypt, Babylon and India – decided to add Greece to his list of conquests. But the Greeks, armed only with javelins and swords, defeated the mighty Persian army. A messenger was sent to take the good news to Athens. Upon completing his 40-kilometre (26-mile) run, legend says he delivered his message, collapsed and died. Today, the marathon event in athletics commemorates the messenger's journey.

The most decorated unit in US military history was formed primarily of Japanese-Americans.

While testing a newly compiled computer programme, US Government workers found a real-life Donald Duck. The programmers used this made-up name to test their military software but found out there was an army engineer with that name. The soldier became famous and was a guest on the Johnny Carson TV show as a result of this discovery.

Many different tribes lived in Roman Britain. If they had spent less time fighting each other and more time fighting the Romans, they might have won. British warriors sometimes fought their battles naked, dyed blue from head to toe. They also bleached their long hair until it was white and so stiff that it stood on end in long hard points.

PART 2
CRIME FACTS

LOOPY LAWS

Some Very Strange Laws

In New Mexico, USA, women are strictly forbidden to appear unshaven in public.

According to a British law passed in 1845, attempting to commit suicide was a crime punishable by the death penalty.

An old Boston law requires that you must get a prescription to take a bath.

A New York state law declared that any person riding in a lift cannot talk to anyone, and must keep his or her eyes looking forwards at the elevator door at all times with their hands in a folded position until they leave.

In England in 1571, a man could be fined for not wearing a wool cap.

In Florida, USA, women can be fined for falling asleep under a hair dryer, as can the salon owner for letting them.

In Fairbanks, Alaska, it is illegal for a moose to be on the pavement. This dates back to the early days of the town when the owner of a bar had a pet moose that he used to get drunk. The moose would then stumble around the town inebriated. The only way the authorities could prevent this from happening was to create the law stopping the moose from crossing the pavement to get access to the bar.

In Sparta during the 4th century BC, if you were male and over 20 years of age, you were required by law to eat two pounds of meat a day. It was supposed to make you brave.

It is against the law to whale hunt in Oklahoma, a landlocked American state.

In the 16th century, King François I of France made the wearing of whiskers punishable by death.

Massachusetts in the US has a law that prohibits using bullets as a form of currency.

Also in Massachusetts, state laws decree that mourners at a gathering after a funeral may not eat more than three sandwiches, and that snoring is prohibited unless all your bedroom windows are closed and securely locked. Plus ... an old law declares goatee beards to be illegal unless you first pay a special licence fee for the privilege of wearing one.

Posting a building has been illegal in the US since 1916 when a man mailed a 40,000-ton brick house across Utah to avoid freight rates.

In Nebraska, USA, a parent can be arrested if his child cannot hold back a burp during a church service.

Hypnotism is banned in public schools in San Diego, USA.

In the US town of Grants Pass, Oregon, you can throw onions at "obnoxious salesmen" if they won't stop knocking on your door.

By law, in Bourbon, Missouri, USA, one small onion must be served with each glass of water in a restaurant.

In Tamarack, Idaho, in the US, you can't buy onions after dark without a special permit from the sheriff.

In Somalia, Africa, it is illegal to carry old chewing gum stuck on the tip of your nose.

In the American state of Utah, birds have the right of way on all highways.

The sale of chewing gum is outlawed in Singapore because it is a means of "tainting an environment free of dirt".

In Finland, people must be able to read in order to get married.

In Greece, if you are unbathed or poorly dressed while driving on the public roads of Athens, you may have your driving licence taken away.

It is against the law for a woman weighing over 200 pounds and wearing shorts to be seen eating onions in a restaurant or at a public picnic in Ridgeland, South Carolina, USA.

By law, no shop is allowed to sell a toothbrush on the Sabbath in Providence, Rhode Island, USA. Yet these same shops are allowed to sell toothpaste and mouthwash on that day.

According to a 1649 Massachusetts law, punishment for stubbornness in children over the age of 16 was death.

In 1837 a British judge ruled that if a man kissed a woman against her will she was legally allowed to bite his nose off.

In Hartford, Connecticut, USA, you may not, under any circumstances, cross the street walking on your hands.

In Sarasota, Florida, USA, it's illegal to sing in a public place while attired in a swimsuit, and men may not be seen publicly in any kind of strapless gown.

In Chester, England, you can only shoot a Welsh person with a bow and arrow inside the city walls and after midnight.

In Switzerland, it is illegal to flush the toilet after 10 p.m. if you live in a flat.

In Gainesville, Georgia, USA, it is illegal to eat chicken with a fork.

A law in International Falls, Minnesota, USA, makes it illegal for cats to chase dogs up telephone poles in the city.

It is illegal to cross the state boundaries of Iowa with a duck on your head.

During the great plague in the 14th century, a law was passed that people should say "God bless you" to anyone who sneezed. At the time it was believed that the sneezes were a way of expelling evil from the body.

In Cleveland, Ohio, USA, it's illegal to catch mice without a hunting licence.

In Utah, USA, it is illegal to swear in front of a dead person.

In the 1940s, Californian law made it illegal to dress as a member of the opposite sex. Drag queens avoided the restriction by attaching pieces of paper to their dresses which read "I'm a boy". The courts accepted the argument that anyone wearing such a notice was technically dressed as a man, not a woman.

It is against the law to remove your shoes if your feet smell bad while you're in a theatre in Winnetka, Illinois, USA.

During the reign of Catherine I of Russia, men weren't allowed to get drunk before nine o'clock. And ladies weren't allowed to get drunk at all.

In Blue Hill, Nebraska, USA, no woman wearing a "hat which would scare a timid person" can be seen eating onions in public.

It was illegal for women to wear buttons in 15th-century Florence.

In Florida, a special law prohibits unmarried women from parachuting on Sundays. And if an elephant is left tied to a parking meter, the parking fee has to be paid just as it would for a vehicle.

In Milan, Italy, there is a law that requires a smile on the face of all citizens at all times. Exemptions include time spent visiting patients in hospitals or attending funerals. Otherwise, the fine is £60.

In Massachusetts, USA, it is illegal to go to bed without first having a full bath.

Women were banned by royal decree from using hotel swimming pools in Jiddah, Saudi Arabia, in 1979.

Texas is the only state in the US that permits residents to vote from space. The first to exercise this right to vote while in orbit was astronaut David Wolf, who cast his vote for Houston mayor via e-mail from the Russian space station Mir in November 1997.

A law in Harper Woods, Michigan, USA, makes it illegal to paint sparrows for the purpose of selling them as parakeets.

It was once against the law to slam your car door in cities in Switzerland.

In Kentucky, USA, anyone who has been drinking is legally "sober" until he or she "cannot hold onto the ground". Also, it is illegal to transport an ice-cream cone in your pocket.

Reportedly, in Saudi Arabia a woman may divorce her husband if he does not keep her supplied with coffee.

An old law in Jonesboro, Georgia, USA, made it illegal to use the expression "Oh, boy!" This came about because a man who lived in Jonesboro, who was elderly and wealthy, would often hire young boys to do work for him by calling out to them, "Oh, boy!" Some teenagers started to shout "Oh, boy!" every time they saw him. The man got fed up with this and, as he had quite a bit of influence in the community, he had the law passed that made it illegal to say "Oh, boy!" in public. However, the teenagers had the last laugh. When they saw him in public after that, one of them would yell, "Oh ..." and another would yell, "... boy!"

In the US town of Lexington, Kentucky, women cyclists cannot wear a swimsuit unless they're escorted by two policemen.

NOT A SHOPPING LIST

America's Most Wanted

America's Most Wanted Criminals list started in 1949, when a reporter wrote a story about the "toughest guys" sought by the Federal Bureau of Investigation. In response, the FBI provided ten names of wanted criminals.

The article created a sensation. Delighted at the subsequent publicity, FBI Director J. Edgar Hoover began the Ten Most Wanted Fugitives programme in March 1950. Since then the list has become a standard crime-fighting tool for the FBI. By widely circulating the lists to the media, the FBI has been able to enlist public help in finding what it calls "serious offenders".

Of the 458 names that have appeared on the list, 429 have been apprehended, including 137 as a direct result of tips from the public.

At first, bank robbers, burglars and car thieves dominated the list. In the 1960s, more fugitives were charged with destruction of property, sabotage and kidnapping. As organised crime and political terrorism increased in the 1970s, the make-up of the list changed again, and today, organised crime bosses, drug dealers, terrorists and serial killers dominate. To be on the list, a suspect must be especially dangerous, and authorities must believe that publicity would increase the chances of arrest.

Fugitives stay on the list until they are captured, or the charges against them are dropped, or they are no longer a menace to society, or they die.

YO HO HO!

Pirate Facts & Funnies

The word "pirate" simply means someone who robs or plunders on the sea. Today piracy is just a term for sea-robbery – any robbery committed under the laws of the Admiralty, rather than the laws of the land.

To stress the point that a pirate's crimes had been committed within the jurisdiction of the British Admiralty, 18th-century pirates were hanged at low-tide mark at Wapping in London. Below the low-tide mark counted as Admiralty territory; anything above it was for the civil courts to deal with.

As far back as the 6th century BC, pirates were robbing trading ships in ancient Greece.

The Roman Empire battled constantly against pirates stealing their grain imports.

In the 1500s, the Barbarossa (Redbeard) brothers, Aruj and Kheir-ed-din, roamed the Mediterranean. These "corsairs" were feared throughout the Mediterranean for their ferocious attacks on Christian ships and coastal settlements.

In the 16th century, British "privateers" such as Sir Francis Drake and Sir John Hawkins attacked Spanish galleons and relieved them of looted treasures from South America in the name of the British crown. "Letters of Marque" were issued to privateers by the British, permitting them to rob the Spanish whenever they could. The success of their voyages encouraged others, who didn't restrict their attacks to Spanish ships but took any vessel that might hold a valuable cargo. King James I withdrew all the Letters of Marque in 1603.

Scotland has made its contribution to the fact and fiction surrounding the pirate:

Scottish writers have played a major role in the development of pirate mythology. J.M. Barrie wrote the tale of *Peter Pan*, taking many of the characteristics of the evil Captain Hook from the notorious real-life pirate, Blackbeard. Robert Louis Stevenson wrote the classic *Treasure Island*, which features the most famous fictional pirate of all: Long John Silver. There have been real-life Scottish pirates, too: in the 18th century, a Scottish sixpence was recovered from the wreck off the American coast of pirate Black Sam Bellamy's flagship, the *Whydah*, which indicated that the pirate crew was at least partly Scots.

The classic pirate era continued into the 18th century when many of the most notorious buccaneers roamed the seas. The two women pirates, Mary Read and Anne Bonny, were active between 1710 and 1720; Black Sam Bellamy roamed the coast of colonial America from early 1716 to mid 1717; and the infamous Blackbeard was killed in 1718 after two years of terrorising Caribbean seafarers.

Privateers made a comeback during the American Revolution (1775–83) when hundreds boosted the small American Navy and attacked English merchant ships, crippling trade. Scottish-born John Paul Jones' daring raids on behalf of the American Navy made him an American national hero.

For 30 years, from 1690 to 1720, the island of Madagascar was the principal base of the pirates preying on the rich trade of the Indian Ocean. Barely explored, Madagascar was the ideal hiding place for pirates driven out of the Caribbean.
A visitor at the end of the 17th century counted 17 pirate vessels and an estimated population of 1,500 buccaneers.

By the beginning of the 19th century, navies no longer needed the help of the privateers. The introduction of steam-powered ships meant that pirates could be easily pursued and caught. It was the beginning of the end for the buccaneers.

Today, piracy has been largely wiped out along the main trade routes but in Southeast Asia and some parts of the Caribbean, piracy is still alive and well. The same cannot be said of some of their victims.

It was common for arguments to arise on long passages at sea. Strict rules were used to settle these disputes and ensure that booty was equally shared. Rules varied from ship to ship, but here is one pirate captain's example of a rulebook:

1. Every man shall obey command.

2. The captain shall have one full share and a half in all prizes.

3. The master, carpenter, boatswain and gunner shall have one share and a quarter.

4. Any man wishing to leave ship shall be marooned, with a bottle of powder, a bottle of water, one small arm, and shot.

5. Every man has a vote in all affairs.

6. No person to gamble aboard ship at cards or dice for money.

7. No striking on board, but every quarrel to be ended on shore, by sword and pistol.

8. No boy or woman is to be allowed among the crew.

The pirate flag was designed to strike fear into victims and encourage a hasty surrender. However, the black Jolly Roger commonly associated with pirates was not as greatly feared as the red flag, which meant that no mercy would be shown in battle. The Jolly Roger often depicted symbols of death and may have got its name from a nickname for the devil – Old Roger – but is more likely derived from the French name for the red flag – Jolie Rouge.

Pirates lived in times when navigation was primitive and printed maps were not widely available. To be successful, pirates had to position themselves across the known trade routes. After taking a prize, the pirates would flee to a bolthole, perhaps the island of Madagascar or some tiny Caribbean islet. Maps and navigational tools were vital and often the most valuable booty captured from the victim ships.

The cutlass evolved from the knives used by the original buccaneers to cut meat for barbecues. Its short blade made it ideal for use in confined spaces and it was the favoured weapon of nearly all pirates.

With its shortened barrel, the musketoon wasn't accurate, but it was easy to use on board where enemies were close and accuracy was not essential. It was the gun of choice for the discerning buccaneer.

The flintlock was light and the ideal weapon for boarding a victim ship. But if the powder got damp, the gun wouldn't fire, and it could fire only one shot at a time. So a pirate would carry several, and use them as clubs when all his bullets had gone.

A boarding axe was used to climb the sides of a ship. Once on deck, the axe could bring down sails to prevent escape.

When they reached a port, pirates liked to party, spending an absolute fortune on drink and gambling. But there is no rest for the wicked, and there was a lot of hard work to be done before they could sail again. The ship had to be serviced, which meant "careening" – the awful job of scraping all the barnacles off the hull. The sails and rigging had to be repaired and replaced, while other crew members would have the job of finding fresh water and food for the next voyage, which might be several months long. And, of course, there was treasure to bury!

Although the rewards of piracy could be great, the punishment for convicted pirates was to "dance the hempen jig", a pirate term for being hanged. The hanging was a public event which, in London, always took place at Execution Dock at Wapping.

Convicted pirates were taken from prison in a procession led by an officer carrying a silver oar – the symbol of the Admiralty – to the gallows at the low-tide mark. After a sermon from the chaplain, the pirate could address the crowd before execution. After execution, the bodies were left until three tides had washed over them, as a warning to others.

The preservation of food was a major problem for pirates, or indeed any seafarers of the time, before the invention of refrigeration and canned goods. Bottles of beer were preferred over water, which quickly became undrinkable. The staple food was "hard tack" – horrible hard biscuits. For very long voyages, limes would provide vitamin C to prevent scurvy, and hens on board the ship could provide both fresh eggs and meat. The main source of meat in the Caribbean were turtles, which could be picked up on any beach; they made for good eating.

The cat o' nine tails was a whip with many lashes, used for flogging lawbreakers on board a pirate ship. A "taste of the cat" might be a full flogging, or just a single blow to "smarten up" an unruly deckhand.

Keelhauling was the hideous punishment of dragging a man under the ship with ropes, from one side to the other. The victim of a keelhauling would be half-drowned, or worse, and lacerated by the barnacles that grew on the ship's hull. Walking the plank is the most famous piratical execution, beloved of makers of pirate-themed movies for a century. The victim, usually blindfolded and with bound hands, is forced to walk along a plank laid over the ship's side, until he falls into the water below. This punishment first appeared in 19th-century fiction, long after the great days of piracy, and is thought not to have been practised in reality.

YOUR MONEY OR YOUR LIFE

The Ways of Highwaymen

Highwaymen were common in England from the 14th century, when the country was pretty lawless. There were several peaks in their numbers however: just after the English Civil War (1642–1649) when soldiers from disbanded armies took to the road, and between 1697 and 1701, when the same happened with soldiers returning from the wars in France. The real golden age, however, was between 1700 and 1800, when it was rare not to be attacked on the road and many people actually wrote their wills before setting off on a coach trip.

Many highwaymen were of gentlemanly birth. There was little shame at the time in being recognised as a highwayman, and to be robbed by a famous one was regarded as something of an honour.

Victims were mostly the wealthy, and highwaymen were popular with the common folk, who didn't mind about the rich gentry getting held up. Highwaymen had a reputation for generosity with their loot, so they could usually be assured of a warm reception at the inns and pubs they visited.

By the end of the 18th century, the heyday of the English highwaymen was about over. Faster coaches, more traffic and better roads made holding up travellers trickier. Pub landlords were refused licences if they were known to harbour highwaymen, and the Government started posting horse patrols along the approach roads to London.

DICK TURPIN

Legend or Lightweight?

Dick Turpin's most famous and daring exploit was a ride from London to York on his faithful mare, Black Bess, in less than 24 hours. But it isn't true. This great ride was made by another highwayman, John "Swift Nick" Nevison, who made the ride of more than 190 miles in 15 hours to establish an alibi. It was attributed to Turpin in a novel and repeated in magazines, cheap novels and ballads.

Even today, there are so many inns along the Great North Road that boast Dick Turpin stopped there for a drink on his epic ride, he would have fallen off his horse long before he reached York!

Though Dick Turpin is often thought of today as the image of the dashing, gallant highwayman, he was little more than a burglar, a murderer and a horse thief.

Born in 1706 in rural Essex, Turpin served an apprenticeship with a butcher. When he had served it, he opened his own butcher's shop, and began to steal sheep, lamb and cattle as a sideline to fill his shelves. Caught in the act of stealing two oxen, he fled into the Essex countryside, where he tried his hand at smuggling. There he became a member of the notoriously vicious Essex Gang, an appalling bunch who started out as deer-rustlers before branching out into looting churches and robbing farmhouses. It was only after most of the gang were hanged, when one of their number gave them up to the police, that Turpin took to the road, at first in company with another highwayman,

"Captain" Tom King. King and Turpin worked in Waltham Forest, robbing passers-by. By 1737, Turpin had a £200 bounty on his head. The partnership came to an end when Turpin stole a horse that was tracked to the Red Lion pub in Whitechapel. When King came to collect the stolen animal, he was arrested. Turpin, waiting nearby, fired at the constables holding King, but he was a terrible shot and managed to shoot King instead. Turpin fled for Yorkshire, where he started horse-dealing under the name John Palmer.

He came to the attention of the local authorities when he shot his landlord's rooster, and threatened to do the same to the landlord. While he was held in custody, he was identified by his former schoolmaster as being none other than the notorious highwayman Dick Turpin himself. Convicted on two charges, Turpin was hanged at York on 19 April, 1739.

PLUNKET AND MACLAINE

The Prince and the Pauper

Plunket and MacLaine were the subjects of a movie in the 1990s, but they were not fictional creations.

James MacLaine lived by day as a gentleman in London's St James's, while his accomplice, William Plunket, lived nearby in rather more humble circumstances. MacLaine was born in 1742, the son of a minister in the north of Ireland. He took his father's inheritance to Dublin where, aged 18, he blew the lot on gambling and women. Shunned by his family, he moved to England, married an innkeeper's daughter and set up as a grocer. When his gambling ruined the business and his wife died, he struck up the famed criminal partnership with fellow bankrupt, Plunket. With stolen pistols and horses and their faces hidden by Venetian masks, they had a short but highly successful career as highwaymen. Despite rickety beginnings (MacLaine fled from their first robbery), the pair committed around 20 hold-ups in six months, often in Hyde Park, and claimed many famous victims.

During the hold-up of politician and writer Horace Walpole, MacLaine managed to shoot him accidentally, but the next day he wrote him a very polite letter apologising for any inconvenience caused.

The robberies were always conducted in a restrained and courteous fashion, earning MacLaine the "gentleman highwayman" tag and giving him enough money finally to live the society lifestyle he'd always craved. Actually most of the credit for their success should go to Plunket, as MacLaine was something of a coward who preferred to pursue women rather than wave a pistol about.

MacLaine was arrested when he tried to sell a very distinctive coat that he'd stolen from one Lord Elgington. The coat was recognised and MacLaine was caught.

Such was MacLaine's fame among the fashionable that his trial at the Old Bailey court was a social occasion, and in Newgate prison he reputedly received several thousand visitors, among them many high-society ladies attracted by his dangerous reputation. He was hanged in front of a crowd at Tyburn on 3 October, 1750.

Despite being blamed by his partner for every crime they had committed, Will Plunket was smart enough to escape with both his money ... and his life.

CLAUDE DUVAL

A Pleasure to be Robbed By

Claude Duval was French, born in 1643. He came to England with Royalists returning after the restoration of Charles II to the throne. By 1666 he had picked up a new trade: highway robbery.

His reputation as a dashing sort grew and was soon so widespread that some of his lady victims were actually delighted to be robbed by him. In 1670, Duval held up a coach containing a nobleman and his lady. To show she wasn't afraid, the lady took out a pipe and played a tune. Cheeky Duval asked her to dance, and afterwards relieved her husband of four hundred pounds. Taking a hundred, he gave the rest back to the lady in return for the dance. He became a romantic hero, though his capture was not quite as glorious. He was apprehended at a pub in London, and sent to Newgate prison, where he was tried by judge Sir William Morton. Despite efforts by the ladies of the court, and even the King himself, Sir William refused to change his death sentence. Duval was hanged on 21 January 1670.

He faced his end bravely, before an audience of screaming ladies – many of noble birth – wearing masks to disguise themselves.

Following a grand funeral at St Paul's Cathedral, Duval is said to have been buried beneath the aisle, with the following epitaph:

"Here lies Du Vall: Reader, if male thou art, Look to thy purse. If female, to thy heart. Much havoc has he made of both; for all men he made to stand, and women to fall."

SIXTEEN-STRING JACK

The Dandy Highwayman

John Rann, also known as "Sixteen-string Jack", was born in Bath in the 18th century. He worked as a pedlar, a household servant, a stable lad and, lastly, as a coachman, when he became something of a fashion victim. He began wearing the sixteen ribbons tied at his knees for which, as a highwayman, he was to become famous. In September 1774, Rann was arrested for robbery. At his trial he wore a new suit of pea green, a hat with silver strings, a ruffled shirt – and a smile. Though he expected to be acquitted, when the death sentence was passed he remained composed. The night before he died he threw a party for himself and seven girls!

CRIME AND PUNISHMENT

Olde Worlde Justice

In ancient China, the punishment for shoplifting was to brand the offender's forehead with an iron. Thieves had their noses cut off and drunks were strangled.

In Rhode Island, USA, in 1771, William Carlisle was convicted of passing forged dollars. He was sentenced to have both his ears cut off and to be branded on both cheeks with the letter R for "Rogue".

The Ducking Stool was a medieval method of punishment for nags and brawlers, who were sat in a chair fixed to beams and hung over a pond to be plunged into the water as often as their sentence directed.

"Red Letters" were a way of shaming wrongdoers of old. A letter, cut out of cloth, was sewn onto the wrongdoer's clothing. "V" stood for "viciousness", "A" for adultery, "D" for public drunkenness. The victim had to wear the letter for as long as the sentence decreed, sometimes for life. Anyone caught out and about without their letter on could expect to be publicly whipped.

Medieval thieves and drunkards were put in the stocks – a wooden bench with leg-irons – in the village square for people to mock.

Dishonest traders were put in a pillory – a board with holes for the head and hands. Passers-by could throw dung at them.

A "Scold's Bridle" was an iron cage fitted round the head and into the mouth of a nagging wife to keep her quiet. Some had spiked tongue plates for added discomfort.

OLD BILL

Police Facts & Figures

British police have many nicknames, one of which is "Old Bill". According to Scotland Yard, there are several possible reasons why:

Kaiser Wilhelm I of Prussia visited England around the time, in 1864, when the police uniform changed from top hat and swallowtail coat to helmet and tunic. His nickname was Kaiser Bill.

An "old bill" was, in Victorian times, any banknote presumed to be presented to the police for a bribe to persuade them to turn a blind eye to some criminal activity.

New laws for the police to enforce all come from "Bills" passed through Parliament.

Many police officers wore moustaches like that adorning a famous cartoon character, "Old Bill, the wily old soldier in the trenches" created by Bruce Bairnsfather. In 1917, the Government used Bairnsfather's character in posters and advertisements putting over wartime messages under the heading "Old Bill says". For this campaign, the character was dressed in a special constable's uniform.

Old Bill might refer to the Bill Bailey of an old music hall song "Won't You Come Home, Bill Bailey?" The Central Criminal Court is called the Old Bailey.

The London County Council at one time registered all police, fire and ambulance vehicles with the letters BYL.

Robert Peel was behind the law creating the first police force in England. In 1829, his Metropolitan Police Act was passed by the Government. It applied only to London.

London's police were the responsibility of the Home Secretary, with headquarters at Scotland Yard. A thousand men were recruited, and being a policeman became a full-time job with a uniform and weekly pay of 16 shillings.

"Bobbies" or "Peelers" (nicknames that came from Robert Peel) were not popular. Most citizens viewed constables as interfering busybodies, and people often jeered the police. The police were successful though, and crime and disorder declined.

But while central London's crime-rate fell, that of nearby areas increased. Wandsworth became known as "black" Wandsworth because of all the criminals who lived there.

The police in Portland, Oregon, USA, are helped by a pot-bellied pig called Harley, who has been trained to sniff out illegal drugs and guns.

DUMB CRIMINALS

Truly Stupid Criminals

In 1997, a man in North Carolina, USA, broke into a bank's basement through a window, cutting himself in the process. He found that he could neither reach the money from where he was, nor get out of the window through which he had entered. So he thought for a while, then called the police.

In Messina, Italy, Furio Romano snatched a gold chain from around a woman's neck and sprinted away down the street. He stuffed the chain in his mouth as he ran, accidentally sucked the necklace down his windpipe and fell choking to the ground. Luckily for him the cops were close behind and saved his life before arresting him.

A pair of Michigan, USA, robbers entered a record shop nervously waving revolvers. The first one shouted, "Nobody move!" When his partner moved, the first bandit, startled, shot him.

A man walked into a store in Los Angeles, put a 20-dollar bill on the counter and asked for change. When the clerk opened the cash drawer, the man pulled a gun and asked for all the cash, which the clerk promptly gave him. The man took the cash from the clerk and fled, leaving the 20-dollar bill on the counter. The total amount of cash he got from the drawer? Fifteen dollars.

In Oslo, Norway, in 2003, a burglar picked the wrong apartment to rob. The flat was the one used for Norway's version of *Big Brother*. He was filmed by 17 video cameras which recorded his every move and the whole thing was shown live on the internet.

In Nottinghamshire, a girl snatched a woman's purse containing a little cash and a mobile phone. A short time later, the woman's husband decided to call the phone's number. Someone answered the phone but didn't say anything. In the background the husband heard someone order a Big Mac, so he went to the nearest McDonald's and once inside, called again. The phone rang and this time the husband was close enough to see the thief pick it up and answer. She gave up the phone and the purse without a fight.

Shawn West from New Jersey, USA, was trying to rob a sweets and drinks kiosk on the coast. The kiosk was protected by a metal roller door, and Shawn was fashionably dressed in a pair of extremely baggy jeans. When West broke the lock, the door of the stand went up, catching on his jeans. In the morning, the cops found the 17-year-old high up in the air.

GALWAY COUNTY LIBRARIES

171

In Chicago, USA, Thomas Ingram and two friends broke into a closed restaurant and managed to escape with an automatic cash machine. They squeezed it into the back seat of their car, leaving the back door half open and the machine partially hanging out. Not surprisingly, this attracted a police officer who pulled them over and arrested them. He was able to inform them that the cash machine had been out of order and empty of cash for two years – the restaurant owner had been trying to figure out how to get rid of it.

In Launceston, Australia, a gang tried to rob a cash machine in a shopping centre. They had stolen some welding equipment, which they used to cut open the machine. After several minutes of work, the money in the machine burst into flames and was reduced to ashes.

In 1998, Jason Emmons walked into a corner shop in Tennessee, USA, with a shotgun and demanded all of the money from the till. After the cashier put the money in a bag, the man demanded a bottle of whisky he saw behind the counter. The cashier refused to hand it over because he didn't believe the man was old enough to drink alcohol. Finally, the robber handed over his ID and proved that he was 21. After he left, the cashier called the police and gave them the robber's name and address. Jason was arrested two hours later.

In Indiana, USA, Christopher Adams was pulled over for a minor traffic offence. While talking to him, the officer couldn't help but notice his bright orange T-shirt which read, "Fugitive. You never saw me". He ran Adams' name through the computer and, sure enough, he was indeed a fugitive, wanted for failure to appear at a court hearing. Adams went to jail.

In Mount Shasta, California, Joy Glassman was a loving mother who wanted her sons to get on in life, but she went too far. Her sons grew up to be firemen, and Joy deliberately set fires to help their careers. In 1995, after the fifth one, she was arrested.

In Texas, USA, Andre Meyers held up a convenience store, getting away with some cash and fleeing on foot. He ran to a nearby car park where his getaway car and driver were waiting. They sped away – for about seven metres (20 feet), before they ran out of petrol. They were still trying to re-start the car when the police arrived.

In Mexico City, a man entered a bakery at eight one morning, flashed a knife and demanded a slice of chocolate cake. He enjoyed it so much he was back the next morning for more. And the next day. And the next. On the fifth day the police were waiting for him.

In London, Andrew Collins stole a woman's bank debit card. He headed to the local betting shop where he used the card to place two bets on horse races. Both his horses came in and he won £300. But, since he'd used a debit card and couldn't show proper ID, the betting shop simply paid the winnings into the debit card account rather than paying him in cash as he had expected. The woman whose card was stolen actually ended up £300 better off, and the thief was arrested.

During Prohibition, the consumption of alcohol was banned in the United States. A jury for an illegal alcohol smuggling, or "bootlegging", case in Los Angeles was put on trial after it drank the evidence. The jurors argued that they had sampled the evidence to determine if it contained alcohol, which it did.
However, because they had consumed the evidence, the defendant charged with bootlegging had to be acquitted.

In California, a man robbing a bank demanded that the clerks give him all the money. They asked him to go and sit in his car and they would bring the money out. He agreed. The people in the bank called the police, and when they got there he was still sitting in his car waiting. They arrested him.

In Missouri, USA, Michael Massey was caught trying to steal six 160-kilogram (350-pound) transformers from a local power company. He said he needed them to power a time machine he was building in order to travel into the future and get the lottery numbers.

In ancient Greece, a statue was built of a famous boxer named Theagenes after his death. A jealous rival attacked the statue one night and it fell over and killed him. The dead man's family took the statue to court, where it was found guilty of murder and thrown out of the country.

In Hitachi, Japan, a robber burst into a shop armed with a knife and demanded cash. In the middle of the robbery he realised he'd forgotten to wear his mask. Realising that without it capture was almost certain, he put away his weapon and asked the shopkeeper to please call the police. The shopkeeper did so and the robber explained his predicament to the police, asking them to come over and arrest him as soon as conveniently possible. They were glad to do so.

In Penrith, Australia, a gang smashed their truck through the window of a petrol station. Then they attached a chain to the cash machine inside. They connected the chain to the rear of their truck and sped away. As they dragged the heavy machine through the city streets, sparks flew from under the machine, eventually setting fire to the truck. The gang bailed out before the truck exploded.

A 27-year-old man in New York broke into a house and decided he liked a pair of trousers he found in there better than the ones he was wearing, so he got changed. Police tracked him down after they found his name and address in the pocket of the jeans he had left behind.

In Idaho, USA, a woman's getaway was ruined when she ran out of the shop she had just robbed and jumped into what she thought was a taxi. It was a police car.

In Bucharest, Romania, two burglars put the socks they were wearing on their hands to avoid leaving behind any fingerprints when they robbed a phone shop. The socks smelled so strongly that a police dog was able to track them from the shop all the way to their hiding place, and they were under arrest less than two hours later.

Nolan Preston broke into a hospital in Wiltshire and stole some pagers. Then he spotted a tanning bed. Feeling a little pale, he jumped in and set the timer for 45 minutes. Unfortunately for him, this was not a tanning bed but a special ultra-violet light machine for burn victims and only supposed to be used for ten seconds at a time. Preston was arrested by the police when he arrived to be treated for his injuries at a second hospital, still wearing the doctor's coat he had stolen from the first.

In Bath, England, two thieves snatched the purse of Pamela McCarthy and ran off down the street. What they didn't know was that 40-year-old Pamela was a marathon runner and she chased them for more than a mile before they finally ran into their house. She then called the police who came over and arrested them.

A convicted burglar was being escorted to jail in Florida, USA, when he managed to break loose and flee. During his escape, he suffered a number of cuts on his feet, but was still able to outrun the cops. Police searched the area but the man had completely vanished. However, they got a break in the case when the local hospital called to say that they were treating a man who might be a fugitive. It seems that the escapee had filled out his hospital form giving the "reason or cause of injury" as "escape from jail".

A judge in Kentucky, USA, decided a jury went "a little bit too far" in recommending a sentence of 5,005 years for a man who was convicted of five robberies and a kidnapping. The judge reduced the sentence to 1,001 years.

In Bruno d'Asti, Italy, Carlo Brunelli held up a post office at gunpoint, fleeing with about £2,500. Postal employees locked the door after Brunelli fled and watched as he got into his car, sat there for a moment and then ran back to the door of the post office. Finding it locked, he began to shout for them to please let him in, as he'd left his car keys on the counter. He was still shouting when the police arrived.

Two men tried to pull the front off a cash machine by running a chain from the machine to the bumper of their pick-up truck. Instead of pulling the front panel off the machine, though, they pulled the bumper off their truck. Scared, they left the scene and drove home – leaving the chain still attached to the machine, which was still attached to their bumper and licence plate.

In Bangkok, Thailand, after stealing a woman's purse, a man ran into a building that he thought was a Buddhist temple. He figured that he couldn't be arrested in there. Unfortunately for him, the building was a police station. He was arrested.

In Michigan, USA, the *Ann Arbor News* reported that a man failed to rob a Burger King because the clerk told him he couldn't open the cash register without a food order. So the man ordered onion rings, but the clerk informed him that they weren't available for breakfast, so the robber left.

In Pittsburgh, USA, Robert Nolan held up two convenience stores in one night. He was confronted and arrested by the police outside his own house the following day. How did the police find him so quickly? His getaway van had "Nolan Plumbing and Heating" written on the side in great big letters.

In Missouri, USA, a gunman robbed a 7/11 shop, but returned the money minutes later because his car wouldn't start. Amazingly, the store clerks came out to the car park and gave the robber's car a push. Police officer David Kuppler commented: "We have a very friendly town out here."

A would-be robber had been casing a Boston, USA, bank for several days, waiting for just the right moment to commit a robbery. He queued for the counter, and as he approached the window, he produced a handgun and announced loudly, "THIS IS A HOLD-UP, NOBODY MOVE!" Much to his dismay, the next five customers in line happened to be armed FBI agents on their lunch breaks, waiting to cash their pay cheques. He quickly surrendered with no shots fired. He had failed to notice the FBI Office, which was right next door to the bank.

In Arizona, USA, Michael Jardine tried to rob a shop with a toy gun, which broke when he dropped it on the floor. He ran off, but later tried to rob a supermarket, spraying a shop assistant with pepper spray and trying to grab cash out of her till. She slammed it shut before he could get the cash, and he started having an asthma attack brought on by his own pepper spray. He struggled to his car only to find he had locked the keys inside. He grabbed a rock, smashed his own window and sped away only to be stopped by the police a few minutes later for driving without his headlights on.

A teenager in New Hampshire, USA, robbed a local convenience store of a couple of pocketfuls of change. He walked home. However, he failed to notice the holes in his pockets, and the trail of dropped change led police directly to his house.

In Rangiora, New Zealand, Michael Burns and his two accomplices made careful plans to break into a tobacco shop. First, they cut the wire leading to the burglar alarm, after which they had all the time in the world to help themselves to cash, cigarettes and even to celebrate with a fine cigar. But before the trio could make their getaway, police were on the scene. The burglar alarm they disconnected was for the shop next door. The one in the tobacco shop was still working just fine.

In Virginia, USA, two men in a pick-up truck went to a new-home site to steal a refrigerator. Bumping into walls, they hauled a fridge from one of the houses and loaded it onto the truck. The truck got stuck in the mud, so the robbers decided that the fridge was too heavy. Bumping into the walls again, they put the fridge back. Returning to the truck, they found that they had locked the keys in it. So they left on foot.

Wayne Black, a suspected thief, had his own name tattooed on his forehead. When confronted by police in April 1998, Black insisted he wasn't Wayne Black. To prove it, he stood in front of a mirror and insisted he was Kcalb Enyaw.

An Indiana, USA, a man told a bystander that he was going to rob a convenience store and gave him a dollar, asking him to go into the store to buy a scarf that he would then use to conceal his identity when he carried out the robbery. The bystander went into the store and used the dollar to call the police.

Surprised while burgling a house in Antwerp, Belgium, a thief fled out of the back door, clambered over a three-metre (nine-foot) wall, dropped down and found himself in the city prison.

In Miami, USA, a man walked into a bank, pulled out his gun and demanded money. After the bank teller filled his bag with loot, the man turned to leave and stuffed the gun back into his pocket. The gun fired, shooting him in the leg. He was able to limp out of the bank and shuffled into the street, where he was hit by a van. He was still able to stagger to his getaway car, but not before spitting out two gold teeth that were knocked loose in the accident. Police tracked him down through his dental records.

Two young car thieves in Florida, USA, appeared before the judge after stealing their 25th car in just two years. After the boys were released, they walked out of the court and discovered they did not have bus fare for a ride home. So the duo stole car number 26, which they crashed into a fence.

In 2003, a man in Zwickau, Germany, broke into a butcher's shop with his dog, Lumpi. He set off an alarm and attempted to run, but Lumpi was still eating sausages when the police arrived and both were apprehended.

In Canberra, Australia, Norman Parker went shopping at a department store and found a sweater he liked. He took it into one of the changing rooms, removed the security tag, stuffed the sweater underneath his jacket and headed for the door. However, the security alarm went off just as he was passing through. How could this have happened? Because when he had removed the security tag, he had put it in his pocket.

In California, USA, a burglar decided that he just couldn't leave without taking a bath in a large bathtub he found. He was still there when the police arrived.

CRIME FILES

Various Criminal Activities

In 2002, a police camera in Gluckstedt, Germany, snapped a duck breaking the speed limit – 39 km/h (24 mph) in a 30 zone.

In Britain, anyone can make a "citizen's arrest". But while the police can arrest a person on suspicion of an offence, other people can only arrest someone they have actually seen committing a crime. Resisting arrest is a crime whether the arrest is made by police or others.

The word "testify" comes from the custom of men in ancient Roman courts swearing to a statement by placing their hand over their testicles.

It was common in the 1930s for gangsters to carry guns wrapped in newspapers. Due to the large size of certain US newspapers in the 1920s and the early part of the 1930s (papers were almost twice the size they are today), even a machine gun could be concealed. Bullets could be fired from guns inside rolled-up newspapers much more efficiently than from a violin case, which is the more usual hiding place in gangster movies.

United States President Franklin Pierce was arrested while in office for running over an old woman with his horse, but the case was dropped due to insufficient evidence in 1853.

The Bible is not only the best-selling book of all time, it is also the book most often stolen from bookshops in the USA.

In England, murder is murder. There are no degrees of murder, as in the United States.

A number of religious groups – for example the Jehovah's Witnesses and the Plymouth Brethren – are not permitted to judge other people's actions, and therefore say that they would be unable to take part in jury decision-making. Excusal on this basis has been permitted by law in the UK only in the last few years – before that, the issue had to be argued every time a juror was summoned.

The Beefeaters who guard the Tower of London are properly called Yeoman Warders. A perk of the job originally was a daily allowance of beer and beef, an expensive luxury out of reach of the ordinary working citizen. "Beefeaters" was a nickname awarded the Warders out of jealousy for their cushy position.

In Kirkland, Illinois, USA, it is illegal for bees to fly over the village or through any of its streets.

The first recorded incident of a drunk-driving conviction was in 2800 BC. In ancient Egypt, an inebriated charioteer was apprehended after running down a vestal virgin of the goddess Hathor. The culprit was crucified on the door of the tavern that sold him the beer, and his corpse allowed to hang there until scavengers had reduced it to bones.

The town council of Gold Hill, Oregon, USA, voted to fire Police Chief Katie Holmboe for selling Mary Kay cosmetics out of her police car and praying on behalf of a suspect she believed was possessed by the devil.

A man in Colorado, USA, was arrested for roller-skating down a steep section of road. He was charged with speeding and running a stop sign. The speed limit was 72 km/h (45 mph).

The expression "daylight robbery" came from highwaymen who held up travellers in broad daylight rather than at night – a very brazen act which was obvious to anyone looking on and made identification of the highwayman easier. It therefore came to mean a blatant and obvious act of theft.

New York was the first American state to require the licensing of motor vehicles. The law was adopted in 1901.

The vast majority of police cars in Britain are white, but in London, red police cars are driven by officers of the Royalty and Diplomatic Protection Group. In addition to close protection of members of the Royal Family, the group is also responsible for the security of foreign embassies and the protection of politicians and diplomats from home or abroad.

In the USA, federal law states that children's TV shows may contain only ten minutes of advertising per hour and on weekends the limit is ten and a half minutes.

Oxford University requires all members upon admission to the Bodleian Library to read aloud a pledge that includes an agreement to not "kindle therein any fire or flame". Regulations also prohibit readers bringing sheep into the library.

Over 16,000 Americans have received new identities under the Federal Witness Security Program.

Bowling used to be done with nine pins. When a law was passed in colonial Connecticut making "bowling at nine pins" illegal, those who ran the games simply started using ten pins.

Temperature and crime are correlated. Many more crimes are committed in the hot summer months than in the cold winter months.

In 1658, Paris police raided a monastery and sent twelve monks to jail for eating meat and drinking wine during Lent.

A stolen car is 200 times more likely to get into a crash than other cars.

Jack the Ripper, the notorious murderer in 19th-century England, committed his crimes only at weekends.

Organised crime is estimated to account for 10% of the United States' entire annual national income.

Half of all crimes in the USA are committed by people under the age of 18, and 80% of burglaries are committed by people aged 13–21.

In Bangkok, Thailand, in 1996, police searched the men's toilets of Thailand's Parliament after an anonymous bomb threat was phoned in. They got a surprise. They found a box they feared contained a bomb, but discovered instead that it contained a monitor lizard. The *Bangkok Post* headline the following day was: "Lizard fails to explode in MPs' toilet".

In the USA, the Eisenhower Interstate System requires that one mile in every five must be straight. These straight sections are usable as airstrips in times of war or other emergencies.

Licenced London taxis (black cabs) are required by law to carry a bale of hay at all times. This dates from the days of the horse-drawn cab, and the law has never been revoked.

A monkey was once tried and convicted for smoking a cigarette in South Bend, Indiana, USA.

In Britain, the law was changed in 1789 to make hanging the method of execution. Prior to that, burning was the usual sentence.

The greatest funeral for a Chicago gangster ever held was for a flower shop entrepreneur named Dion O'Banion. The shop, at the corner of State and Superior Streets, was a front for O'Banion's bootlegging and hijacking operations. Ten thousand mourners were in attendance, and the most expensive wreath – it cost $1,000 – came from Al Capone, who had ordered that O'Banion be killed.

In 1979, 14 children aged ten years old or younger were charged with murder in the United States.

BBC TV's *Crimewatch* **programme shows reconstructions of real crimes to help the police catch real criminals. Soon after watching one** *Crimewatch* **reconstruction, a police officer on duty noticed a man with similar looks and build to the criminal, and attempted to arrest him. He discovered that the man in question was the actor** *Crimewatch* **had employed in the reconstruction.**

In 1861, John Wentworth fired the entire Chicago Police Department when his term as mayor came to an end.
He fired sixty patrolmen, three sergeants, three lieutenants, and one captain. The city was entirely without police protection for twelve hours until the Board of Commissioners swore in new officers.

The murder of a brother is called "fratricide" and murder of a sister, "sororicide".

In 17th-century Japan, no citizen was allowed to leave the country on penalty of death. Anyone caught coming in or going out without permission was executed on the spot.

In Tsu, Japan, a robber marched into a bank and demanded cash. Employees led him to the bank's main vault but when he went inside to grab his cash, they closed the door, locking him inside. And that's where he stayed until the police turned up.

The Tower of London – for which construction was begun in 1078 by William the Conqueror – is currently the home of the British Crown Jewels and is a major tourist attraction. In its time, it has also housed a prison and place of execution, and served as an observatory, a mint, a zoo and a royal palace.

During the time that the atomic bomb was being developed by the United States at Los Alamos, New Mexico, security in the building was very strict and military secrets were under tight protection. So much so that applicants for routine jobs, like cleaners and decorators, were disqualified if they could read. Illiteracy was a legal job requirement.

In Japan, where kissing was considered (by Tokyo's Prefect of Police) to be "unclean, immodest, indecorous, ungraceful, and likely to spread disease", about 240 kilometres (150 miles) of kissing scenes were deleted from US movies released there in 1926.

In most American states, a wedding ring is exempt by law from inclusion among the assets in a bankruptcy estate. This means that a wedding ring cannot be seized by creditors, no matter how much the bankrupt person owes.

In 1967, the CIA fitted a known criminal's pet cat with high-tech listening equipment. Ten minutes after the cat was released, it was run over by a taxi.

In 1671, the notorious spy and wanted outlaw Thomas Blood attempted to steal the Crown Jewels from the Tower of London. He and his gang were captured and imprisoned in the Tower. Blood refused to speak to anyone except King Charles himself, who agreed to see him at Whitehall. On July 18th, 1671, instead of being hanged for treason, Blood was released from his prison cell, had his properties restored to him and was granted a pension of £500 per year by the King. Why King Charles released him remains a mystery to this day.

The country of Togo has the lowest crime rate in the world, with an average of just 11 reported crimes annually for every 100,000 of the population.

BEHIND BARS

Prisoners' Tales

In Belo Horizonte, Brazil, a prisoner escaped on foot from the police jail. He had not gone very far when he saw a bus approaching. He hailed the bus and got on, where he discovered that inside the bus were ten city policemen on their way to look for him. He returned to jail.

Nearly 43% of convicted criminals serving prison sentences in the USA are re-arrested within a year of being released from prison.

There are more people in prison in the United States than there are people living in Tuscon, Arizona.

In the 102 prisons in the USA, 93% of inmates are men. The average age of an inmate is 37, and the most common sentence is 5–10 years.

In Alberta, Canada, prisoner Raymond Tyree tried to pull a daring escape. He crawled into the prison's ventilation system, intending to make his way to an outside wall. Round and round he crawled, avoiding capture but never finding a way out. Other prisoners took pity on him and left him food and water. Eventually, prison officials tracked him down, two months later and 13 kilograms (30 pounds) lighter.

Marie-Augustin Marquis de Pelier was arrested in 1786 and spent the next 50 years in prison. His crime? Whistling at Queen Marie Antoinette as she was being ushered into a theatre.

The slogan on New Hampshire car licence plates in the US is "Live Free or Die". These licence plates are manufactured by prisoners in the state prison in Concord.

Herman Melville, the author of whale story *Moby Dick*, was once imprisoned in Tahiti as a mutineer, but he was able to escape.

In Zephyrhills, Florida, USA, prisoner Korey Hardy stole his orange prison uniform when he was released. He then wore it to a rock concert, where he drew the attention of one of the 200 police officers working as security at the venue. He was escorted back to jail.

Ironically, the maximum security prison in Saint Albans, Vermont, USA, was responsible in 1996 for sending out holiday brochures enticing tourists to visit Vermont.

Yugoslavian prisoner Savo Radovanovic had been waiting for quite some time to be transferred from one jail to another. Thinking things had to be better in the new place, and getting tired of the wait, he decided to take matters into his own hands. He broke out of jail and while police were conducting a nationwide manhunt for him, he turned up at the front gates of the other prison and was apprehended while trying to break in.

The famed Alcatraz prison in San Francisco Bay was first used as a prison by the army during the US Civil War. Numerous escapes were attempted; however, there is no firm evidence that any succeeded. The word "alcatraz" is Spanish for "pelican".

There have been about 30 films made at or about Alcatraz, including *The Rock* (1996), *Birdman of Alcatraz* (1962), and *Escape from Alcatraz* (1979).

**Alcatraz inmates have included gangsters
Al Capone, Machine-gun Kelly and
Floyd Hamilton, the getaway driver
for notorious bank robbers
Bonny and Clyde.**

Queen Elizabeth I of England scratched
the following message on her prison
window using a diamond:
"Much suspected of me,
Nothing proved can be."

**Each week in the United States, the
population of state and federal prison
increases by about 1,000.**

One out of every 43 American prisoners
escapes from prison. 94% are recaptured.

**North Dakota and New Hampshire have
fewer people in jail per head of population
than any other American state.**

IT'S A DIFFERENT LANGUAGE

Criminal Phrases & Codes

Police in the US use ten codes to let each other know what's going on. You may have heard "10-4" meaning "OK", but here are a few others:

10-0	use caution
10-1	cannot receive you
10-2	receive you OK
10-3	stop transmitting
10-4	OK, I acknowledge
10-5	pass on this message
10-7	out of service
10-8	available for incidents
10-9	repeat your transmission
10-10	off duty
10-12	stand by

10-31	crime in progress
10-32	subject with gun
10-33	alarm sounding, emergency
10-34	a riot
10-37	suspicious vehicle
10-39	urgent – use lights and siren
10-40	silent response
10-41	beginning tour of duty
10-42	ending tour of duty
10-49	broken traffic light
10-50	accident
10-52	ambulance needed
10-54	animals on highway
10-67	person calling for help
10-70	fire alarm
10-74	negative
10-77	estimated time of arrival
10-78	need assistance
10-86	officer on duty
10-90	bank alarm
10-98	jail break
11-99	officer needs help

A criminal organisation will sometimes hire gunmen. These are called "goons", "hatchetmen", "torpedoes", or "trigger men".

Opening a safe is a special job among criminals. A "can opener" or "yegg" can open cheap safes, but a "Peterman" uses nitroglycerine, or "soup" to blow the safe.

To Chicago gangsters, a gun could be a "bean-shooter", "gat", "rod" or "roscoe".

Jack Ketch was a well known hangman in old England. When a pirate "Danced with Jack Ketch", he went to the gallows. And "Pieces of Eight"? These were Spanish silver coins worth one peso or eight reales. There were sometimes literally cut into eight pieces, each piece worth one real.

A "Chicago overcoat" was gangster slang for a coffin.

**"BOLO" is short for "Be On the Look Out",
a police alert to watch out for something
or someone.**

Police investigators are experts in collecting
"dactylograms", otherwise known
as fingerprints.

**The Omertà is the Mafia code of silence
and one of the premier vows taken when
being sworn into the "Family". Violation of
the code is punishable by death.**

The "Jaws of Life" is a heavy rescue tool
used by police and emergency services to
pry open vehicles. It is similar in shape to a
pair of pliers, only much larger and driven by
hydraulics or air pressure. It is fully capable
of cutting a car in half.

**When New York policemen have a party,
they call it "Choir Practice".**

A "duffer" is Australian slang for a
cattle thief.

**The Police Radio Alphabet allows cops to
spell words, names and addresses so that
there is no confusion. So "Hotel Echo Lima
Papa" would spell out "Help!"**

ALPHA	**A**	**N**	NOVEMBER
BRAVO	**B**	**O**	OSCAR
CHARLIE	**C**	**P**	PAPA
DELTA	**D**	**Q**	QUEBEC
ECHO	**E**	**R**	ROMEO
FOXTROT	**F**	**S**	SIERRA
GOLF	**G**	**T**	TANGO
HOTEL	**H**	**U**	UNIFORM
INDIA	**I**	**V**	VICTOR
JULIET	**J**	**W**	WHISKY
KILO	**K**	**X**	X-RAY
LIMA	**L**	**Y**	YANKEE
MIKE	**M**	**Z**	ZULU

A STICKY END

Criminals' Undesirable Executions

In 1844, Jonathan Walker was the last person branded in the US as punishment for a crime. He had the initials "SS" branded into the palm of his right hand as punishment for helping American slaves escape to the Bahamas. (The charge against him was "slave stealing".)

The last public execution in America was the hanging of 22-year-old Rainey Bethea at Owensboro, Kentucky in 1936. He had been convicted of murdering a 70-year-old woman. 20,000 people including over 200 sheriffs and deputies from various parts of the USA gathered to watch.

Strange as it may seem, Doctor Joseph Ignace Guillotin wanted to get rid of the death penalty in 18th-century France. Some executions at the time were by "quartering", where a prisoner's limbs were tied to four oxen and the animals driven in different directions, tearing the victim apart. Guillotin wanted a painless capital punishment method, as a step towards banning the death penalty altogether, so he came up with the guillotine, a machine for chopping off heads. Its first use was on April 25, 1792, when highwayman Nicolas Jacques Pelletier lost his head at Place de Grève in Paris. Thousands of aristocrats, including the king, were guillotined during the French Revolution, and the last guillotining took place in Marseilles on September 10, 1977, when the murderer, Hamida Djandoubi, was beheaded.

The last woman to be executed by burning in England was Christian Bowman in 1789. Her crime was making counterfeit coins.

Sir William Wallace, the Scottish rebel portrayed in the film *Braveheart*, was "hanged, drawn and quartered", a horrible execution which involved chopping a person into pieces, preferably while still alive. His head was placed on a pole on London Bridge, his right arm was hung above a bridge in Newcastle, his left arm was sent to Berwick, his right foot and leg to Perth and his left quarter to Aberdeen where it was buried in what is now the wall at St Machar's Cathedral.

In 1941, Josef Jakobs, a German spy, became the last person to be executed in the Tower of London, England.

Sheep theft is still legally a hangable offence in Scotland.

In France in 1740, a cow was found guilty of sorcery and was hanged.

PART 3
INVENTIONS FACTS

ACCIDENTAL SUCCESSES

Inventions that Just Happened

The first match was accidentally invented in 1826 when chemist John Walker had been mixing a pot of potash and antimony with a stick in his workshop. He scraped the stick against the stone floor to remove the blob of dried mixture from the end of his stirrer, and it burst into flames.

In 1598, Dutch eyeglass maker Hans Lippershey was checking some new lenses by holding them up to the window. He discovered that if they were held the correct distance apart, one in front of the other, the image of the view outside became hugely magnified. He had just invented the telescope.

Innkeeper Ruth Wakefield was baking biscuits one day in the 1930s using a recipe that dated back a hundred years or so. She cut up a chocolate bar and put the chunks in the batter, expecting them to melt. She thought she'd be taking chocolate biscuits out of the oven. Instead, what she got were butter biscuits studded with chocolate pieces. Her mistake – chocolate chip cookies – became one of the world's most popular tea-time treats.

Will Keith Kellogg was the man behind the W.K. Kellogg Foundation, founded in 1906. In 1894, he was trying to improve the vegetarian diet of his hospital patients. While searching for a bread substitute, Kellogg accidentally left a pot of boiled wheat to stand on a hot stove. When Kellogg flattened the dried-out wheat with a roller, each grain emerged as a large, thin flake. The flakes turned out to be a tasty cereal. Kellogg had invented cornflakes!

In 1928, scientist Alexander Fleming found that one of the bacteria samples he had left by a window had gone mouldy. On closer examination he found that the mould was dissolving the harmful bacteria. That's how we got penicillin, one of the greatest medical discoveries in history, which helps people around the world recover from infections.

In the early 1940s, engineer James Wright was charged with a task of the utmost importance to the war effort: to develop a cheap substitute for rubber that could be used to produce tyres for military vehicles, gas masks and a whole host of military gear. Wright tackled the task diligently, working night and day to complete his task ... and ended up inventing Silly Putty. Over 200 million plastic eggs, containing 3,000 tons of Wright's Silly Putty, have been sold since 1949.

In 1928, 23-year-old Walter E. Diemer was working for the Fleer Chewing Gum Company in Philadelphia, USA. In his spare time he played around with new recipes. By accident, he made a batch that was less sticky than ordinary gum, and also stretched more easily. He discovered that with a little persuasion the gum could be used to blow bubbles! He took a lump of his new formula to a local shop, and it sold out in an afternoon. The people at Fleer marketed the creation and Diemer taught salesmen to blow bubbles, to demonstrate what made this gum different from other gums. They called it Dubble Bubble. Walter never got royalties from his invention, which would surely have made him a very wealthy man, but he didn't seem to mind. "I've done something with my life. I've made kids happy around the world," he said. "How many people can make that claim?"

While attempting to develop a super strong glue, 3M employee Spencer Silver accidentally developed a glue that was so weak it would barely hold two pieces of paper together. However, his colleague Art Fry had a use for it. Fry sang with his church choir and marked the pages of his hymnal with small scraps of paper that often fell out. He used Silver's glue to hold the papers in place. Today we call these Post-it™ Notes.

A workman who left the soap-mixing machine on too long was responsible for inventing Ivory Soap, one of the world's leading brands. He was so embarrassed by his mistake that he threw the mess in a stream. Imagine his dismay when the evidence of his error floated to the surface! Result: Ivory Soap, the soap that floats. The careless chap had whipped so much air into the mix that his batch of Ivory was lighter than water, making it much easier to find in the bath.

In the 1950s, George de Mestral came home from a walk in the woods to find his jacket covered with cockleburs – little plant pods with tiny spikes. Interested to see how they worked, De Mestral put the cockleburs under a microscope and saw that each spike ended in a little hook. George's curiosity lead him to the invention of Velcro.

Wilson Greatbatch, a medical researcher, was working on a device to record a patient's irregular heartbeat when he accidentally fitted a resistor of the wrong size into the device. The machine started to pulse, stopped, and pulsed again, just like a human heart. After two years of tinkering, Greatbatch had constructed the first implantable pacemaker. He later invented a corrosion-free lithium battery to power it, and millions have benefited since.

In 1942, Percy Le Baron Spencer was working with radar equipment when he noticed that a chocolate bar had melted in his pocket. Testing a theory, he held a bag of unpopped popcorn in front of the machine. It popped. It was a short step from this discovery to the invention of the microwave oven.

In 1982, researchers at a Japanese laboratory used Superglue to fix a crack in a fish tank. The fumes from the Superglue condensed on fingerprints that had been left on the tank, making them clearly visible. This discovery is now used by police forces the world over to catch criminals.

An extremely famous toy was the result of an attempt by engineer Richard James to produce an anti-vibration device for ship instruments. His goal was to develop a spring that would counterbalance the waves that rock a ship at sea. Instead, he invented the Slinky.

A baker named William Russell Frisbee, of Connecticut, USA, came up with a clever marketing idea back in the 1870s. He embossed the family name on the bottom of the tin plates in which his company's pies were sold. The pans were re-usable, so every time a customer baked a home-made pie, it would be stamped with the name Frisbee, reminding them of the pie that came with the tin. Frisbee's pies were sold throughout Connecticut, where, in the 1940s, students at the famous Yale University began flinging the pie tins through the air for sport. Ten years later, in California, Walter Morrison designed a disk for playing catch. It was made by the Wham-O toy company. On a promotional tour of colleges, the Wham-O president saw the pie-plate tossing craze at Yale. Morrison, no slouch at spotting a winning sales trick, called his flying saucer "Frisbee" after the pie plate from Connecticut.

IF AT FIRST YOU DON'T SUCCEED

Inventions that Took a While

A brilliantly successful but incredibly unlucky inventor, a blacksmith named Thomas Davenport, invented the first rotary electric motor. In 1836 he headed out on foot from his Vermont, USA, home to file a patent application at the Patent Office in Washington, D.C. By the time he got there, he had spent all his money and couldn't afford the $30 fee, so he had to turn around and walk all the way home. When he later posted his application with money he'd raised, the Patent Office was destroyed in a fire. He did finally get credit for his invention on February 5, 1837.

Kleenex tissue was originally designed to be a gas mask filter. It was developed at the beginning of World War One to replace cotton, which was then in high demand by army medics as a surgical dressing.

Canadian inventors Chris Haney, Scott Abbott and John Haney struggled for four years to get anyone interested in their new invention – a quiz-based board game. While it took them only 45 minutes to come up with the idea for the game, they lost $45,000 trying to market it before it finally became a hit. The game was called Trivial Pursuit, and eventually it became a massive worldwide success, but not before it took its creators to the brink of bankruptcy. Unemployed artist Michael Wurstlin designed the board and logo for Trivial Pursuit in exchange for five shares in the company. Despite the early failure, by 1986 his shares were valued at two and a half million dollars.

Frank Epperson, then eleven years old, invented the ice lolly by accident. One day little Frank mixed some soda water powder and water, which was a popular drink in those days. He left the mixture on the back porch overnight with the stirring stick still in it. The temperature dropped to a record low that night and the next day Frank took the stick of frozen soda water to show his friends at school. Eighteen years later, in 1923, Frank remembered his frozen soda water mixture and began a business producing "Epsicles" in seven fruity versions. The name was later changed to the "Popsicle". Over three million Popsicle ice lollies are now sold each year.

UP, UP AND AWAY

The Inventions of Flight

1783

First balloon flight. Jacques and Joseph Montgolfier of Annonay, France, sent up a small, smoke-filled balloon.

1784

First powered balloon. General Jean Baptiste Marie Meusnier developed the first propeller-driven balloon – the crew cranking three propellers to give the craft a speed of about five km/h (three mph).

1797

First parachute jump. André-Jacques Garnerin dropped from about 2,000 metres (6,500 feet) over Monceau Park in Paris.

1852

First dirigible (balloon or airship that can be directed). Henri Giffard, a French engineer, flew in a controllable steam-engine-powered balloon from Paris to Trappe.

1900

First zeppelin flight. Germany's Count Ferdinand von Zeppelin flew the first of his long series of rigid-frame airships. It attained a speed of 29 km/h (18 mph).

1903

First successful heavier-than-air machine flight. Aviation was really born at Kitty Hawk when Orville Wright took to the air. He covered 120 feet in twelve seconds. Later that day, in one of four flights, Wilbur stayed up 59 seconds and covered 260 metres (852 feet).

1913

First multi-engined aircraft. Built and flown by a Russian, Igor Ivan Sikorsky.

1914

First aerial combat. In August, Allied and German pilots started shooting at each other with pistols and rifles, unsuccessfully.

1918

First airmail service. Operated for the Post Office by the US Army, the first service started with one round trip a day between Washington, D.C. and New York City.

1929

First rocket-engine flight. Fritz von Opel, a German car maker, stayed aloft in his small rocket-powered craft for 75 seconds.

1931

First flight into the stratosphere. Auguste Piccard, a Swiss physicist, and Charles Knipfer ascended in a balloon from Augsburg, Germany, and reached a height of 15,787 metres (51,793 feet) in a 17-hour flight.

1937

First successful helicopter flight. Hanna Reitsch, a German pilot, flew a Focke FW-61 at Bremen. Ms Reitsch was also the first female civil and military aviation test pilot.

1942

First American jet plane flight. Robert Stanley, chief pilot for Bell Aircraft, flew the Bell XP-59 Airacomet at Muroc Army Base, California, USA.

1944

First production stage rocket-engine fighter plane. The German Messerschmitt Me 163B Komet became operational in June 1944.

1947

First piloted supersonic flight in an aeroplane. Captain Charles E. Yeager, US Air Force, flew the X-1 rocket-powered research plane faster than the speed of sound at Muroc Air Force Base, California, USA.

1952

First jetliner service. The BOAC De Havilland Comet flight started between London and Johannesburg, South Africa.

1958

First transatlantic jet passenger services. BOAC, New York to London, and Pan American, New York to Paris.

1968

Prototype of world's first supersonic airliner. The Soviet-designed Tupolev Tu-144 made its first flight on December 31.

1976

First regularly scheduled commercial supersonic transport flights begin. Air France and British Airways inaugurated Concorde service. Air France flew the Paris–Rio de Janeiro route, and British Airways flew from London to Bahrain.

1977

First successful human-powered aircraft. Paul MacCready was awarded the Kremer Prize for creating the Gossamer Condor, which was flown by Bryan Allen over a five-kilometre (three-mile) course. The super-light craft was pedal-propelled.

1979

First long-distance solar-powered flight. Janice Brown, a former teacher, flew Solar Challenger for ten kilometres (six miles) in Arizona. The craft's engine was powered by the sun.

2001

First solar-powered flight to the edge of space. NASA's solar-powered plane Helios reached an altitude of 30,000 metres (96,500 feet) during a flight over Hawaii, breaking not only the 24,445-metre (80,200-feet) record for propeller-driven aircraft, but the 25,929-metre (85,068-feet) record for all non-rocket aircraft.

WATCHAMACALLITS

How Inventions Got Their Names

"Patent leather" got its name because the process of applying the polished black finish to leather was once patented.

The snorkel was named after the German word for periscope.

Possibly America's most famous sportsman ever was New York Yankees baseball legend Babe Ruth, and one of America's most celebrated chocolate bars is called "Baby Ruth". There is no connection between the two. The bar was named after President Grover Cleveland's daughter, Ruth, and not the baseball player.

A car's instrument panel is called a dashboard. The term dates back to horse and cart days when dashing horses kicked up mud, splashing the passengers riding behind them. The dashboard was invented to protect them.

THE MAN WITH A PLAN

Leonardo da Vinci

Born in 1452, there appears to be no field of knowledge to which Leonardo da Vinci has not made a contribution.

Anatomy, physics, mechanics, writing, engineering, mathematics, philosophy and botany were all advanced by his genius. Leonardo made the first studies of flight in the 1480s. His Ornithopter flying machine was never created, but the modern-day helicopter is based on the concept. He applied his drawing skills to architecture, canal building and weapons design, and worked for the Duke of Milan as a military engineer, inventing weapons and fortifications.

As military engineer and architect to the Pope's son, Cesare Borgia, Leonardo proposed creating a massive wooden bridge across the eight-kilometre- (five-mile-) wide Gulf of Istanbul. The plan seems like fantasy, but modern engineers have determined that it would have been completely sound.

He drew up plans for a bicycle, a helicopter, an "auto-mobile", a steam-powered cannon, waterwheels, and many industrial machines powered by flowing water.

He also devised plans to cover Milan with canals, and sketched a submarine and an unsinkable double-hulled ship, as well as dredgers for clearing harbours and channels.

He became a civil engineer and architect, building bridges and aqueducts, and as a military engineer he was centuries ahead of his time, designing rudimentary tanks, catapults, machine guns and naval weaponry. His creative and visionary inventiveness has yet to be matched.

Some of da Vinci's side projects included: parachutes, underwater breathing devices, ocean rescue equipment, lathes, pumps, water turbines, swing bridges, cranes, street lights, mechanical saws, contact lenses and scissors.

And in his spare time away from inventing, he proposed – unbelievably to most people at the time – that the Earth rotates around the Sun, and he created the first ever textbook of human anatomy, drawn from the real corpses of executed criminals which he cut up and sketched. Oh, and he was one of the greatest painters of his time, creating (among other celebrated works) the *Mona Lisa* – the single most famous painting in history.

WHAT A DOLL!

The Barbie Story

The Barbie Doll was based on a real human being. She was Barbara Handler, the daughter of Ruth and Elliot Handler.

In the early 1950s, Ruth saw that her daughter and her friends liked playing with adult dolls more than baby dolls. Because all the adult dolls then available were made of paper or cardboard, Barbara decided to create a three-dimensional adult female doll. She took her idea to the advertising executives at Mattel Corp., the company that she and her husband, Elliot, had started some years before. The executives rejected the idea as too expensive and with no potential for wide market appeal. Soon after, Barbara returned from Europe with a "Lilli" doll, modelled after a character in a German comic strip. She designed a doll similar to Lilli, hiring a designer to make clothes, and the result was the Barbie. Mattel finally agreed to back it, and Barbie was launched at the New York Toy Fair in 1959.

Barbie set a new sales record for Mattel in her first year on the market: 351,000 dolls, at three dollars each. Today, with over one billion dolls sold, the Barbie product line is the most successful in the history of toys.

Barbie has been joined by friends and family over the years, including Ken (named after the Handlers' son) in 1961, Midge in 1963, Skipper in 1965 and Christie (an African-American doll) in 1968. In 1995, Barbie got a little sister, Baby Sister Kelly (known as Shelly in the UK), and, in 1997, a friend in a wheelchair, Share-a-Smile Becky.

IT'S A HIT!

Toy Hits Through the Century

1900
Baseball cards
1901
Ping-pong
1902
Teddy bear
1909
Jigsaw puzzle
1929
Yo-yo
1933
Monopoly
1943
Scrabble
1957
Frisbee
1959
Barbie doll
1960
Toy Trolls
1971
Space Hopper

1974
Lego
1975
Skateboard
1977
Slime
1980
Rubik's Cube
1983
Cabbage Patch dolls
1989
Nintendo
1990
Rollerblades
1994
Beanie Babies
1996
Buzz Lightyear
1998
Furby
2002
Playstation 2

WHAT'S IN A NAME?
Brand Names that Are the Product

Chapstick	–	Lip balm
Hoover	–	Vacuum cleaner
Kleenex	–	Facial tissues
Rollerblades	–	In-line skates
Sellotape	–	Sticky tape
Styrofoam	–	Plastic foam
Teflon	–	Nonstick coating
Vaseline	–	Petroleum jelly
Velcro	–	Hook and loop fastener
Walkman	–	Portable cassette
Xerox	–	Photocopier

JUST DO IT!

Inventing in Ten Steps

1 Make sketches of your invention.
2 Visit shops. Check out the competition.
3 Find out all about your future customers.
4 Patent your invention. This can cost upwards of £600 and take up to two years. Get an agent if you can afford it.
5 Build and test a small-scale prototype of your invention that demonstrates its uses.
6 Make a plan of how you will make money with your invention.
7 Sell your invention to others or start your own business selling it yourself.
8 Find manufacturers, arrange meetings.
9 Participate at trade shows.
10 Licence your invention to manufacturers and hope your product is a hit!

PATENTLY A GENIUS

Thomas Alva Edison

Thomas Alva Edison (1847–1931) was an American inventor and businessman. He is best known for his invention of the electric light, the phonograph (record player), and movies.

He also started his own newspaper, the *Weekly Herald*, the first paper to be printed and sold on a train. His profits went into setting up his own chemistry lab. When his mother complained of the smell, he moved his lab onto the train as well. Unfortunately, the moving train caused some phosphorous to spill, setting fire to some luggage, and he was asked to leave. So by 1869 he was a full-time inventor. His first idea to receive a patent was the electric vote recorder.

In 1876 he opened a lab in New Jersey. He planned to build a small invention every ten days, and a large invention every six months.

Here he invented the phonograph and the electric light system, and tried to invent the telephone, but Alexander Graham Bell beat him to it. In 1878 he set up the Edison Electric Light Company, and in 1887, he built a new lab in West Orange, New Jersey, where he invented the motion picture camera, the alkaline storage battery, the electric pen (an early printer), and improved the phonograph so that it could be sold commercially.

After his death on October 17, 1931, lights were dimmed for one minute throughout the United States, as a sign of respect and mourning. During his life Edison amassed an incredible 2,332 US and foreign patents.

FOOD, GLORIOUS FOOD

Edible Inventions

New inventions are often called "the best thing since sliced bread", making them the best thing since 1912, when Otto Frederick Rohwedder invented the bread slicer. First he came up with a device that held slices together with hat pins, which was a disaster. In 1928, he designed a machine that both sliced and wrapped.

The original name for French fries was "potatoes, fried in the French manner" – that is how US President Thomas Jefferson first described the dish. Jefferson introduced French fries to the Americans in the late 1700s on his return from diplomatic duties in Europe.

John Montague, Fourth Earl of Sandwich, born in 1718, was the originator of the sandwich. Montague loved to eat beef between slices of toast. He also loved to gamble. The sandwich allowed the Earl to have one hand free for card playing, without having to stop for supper.

The origin of the hamburger is unknown, but the hamburger patty and sandwich were probably brought by 19th-century German immigrants to the United States, where, in a matter of decades, it came to be considered the all-American food. The trademark for the name "cheeseburger" was awarded in 1935 to Louis Ballast of the Humpty Dumpty Drive-In, in Denver, Colorado.

One day in 1853, at Moon Lake Lodge in Saratoga Springs, USA, Cornelius Vanderbilt refused to eat an order of French fries because they were too thick. The chef, George Crum, decided this complaint was unreasonable. To teach the picky diner a lesson, he sliced a potato paper-thin and fried it so heavily it could not be cut with a fork. But Mr Vanderbilt loved them, and potato chips (or crisps) were born.

Caleb Bradham of North Carolina, USA, was a pharmacist. Like many pharmacists at the turn of the century, he had a soda fountain in his shop, where he served his customers refreshing drinks that he created himself. His most popular beverage was created in the summer of 1898. 'Brad's Drink' was made of carbonated water, sugar, vanilla, rare oils, pepsin and cola nuts. The drink was later renamed Pepsi-Cola after the pepsin and cola nuts used in the recipe. In 1940, the first ever nationally broadcast advertising jingle was for Pepsi. The jingle was called "Nickel Nickel" and referred to the price of a can. It became a huge hit record worldwide and was recorded in 55 languages.

The word "ketchup" comes from the Chinese "ke-tsiap", a pickled fish sauce. It made its way to Malaysia where it became "kechap". Heinz began selling tomato ketchup in 1876.

WHAT AND WHEN?

A Brief History of Food Inventions

1872	Blackjack chewing gum
1886	Coca-Cola
1897	Campbell's condensed soup
1898	Shredded Wheat breakfast cereal
1902	Pepsi-Cola
1904	Dr Pepper
1904	Peanut butter
1904	Popcorn
1906	Kellogg's Corn Flakes
1910	Tea bags
1912	Hellmann's mayonnaise
1921	Wrigley's gum
1928	Rice Krispies
1929	Lithiated Lemon (later 7-Up)
1930	Snickers chocolate bar

1936	Mars Bar
1937	Kit Kat chocolate bar
1937	Smarties
1937	Spam
1938	Nescafé (first instant coffee)
1940	McDonald's
1941	Cheerioats (renamed Cheerios in 1946)
1941	M&Ms
1950	Dunkin' Donuts
1954	Burger King
1955	Kentucky Fried Chicken
1958	Pizza Hut
1959	Häagen-Dazs ice cream
1968	McDonald's Big Mac
1969	Sugar-free gum
1971	Starbucks
1977	McDonald's Happy Meals
1982	Diet Coke
1984	Ben & Jerry's ice cream

Around 1500 BC, the Olmec Indians of the Gulf of Mexico were the first to grow cocoa beans as a domestic crop. 2,000 years later, chocolate as a drink became popular among the rich Aztec upper classes, who called it *xocalatl*, meaning "warm or bitter liquid". In 1502, Christopher Columbus encountered a Mayan trading canoe in Guanaja carrying cocoa beans as cargo. Soon afterwards, the drink became popular in Spain, and the Spanish added sugar and vanilla to sweeten the brew. A hundred years later, chocolate rolls and cakes were served in chocolate emporiums all over Europe. In 1795, Dr Joseph Fry of Bristol, England, employed a steam engine for grinding cocoa beans, an invention that led to the manufacture of chocolate on a large scale and, in 1847, Joseph Fry & Son discovered a way to mix the cocoa butter so that it could be moulded. The result was the first modern chocolate bar.

Some names of chocolate bars that were introduced in the 1920s include: Milk Nut Loaf, Fat Emmas, Big Dearos, Vegetable Sandwich, Kandy Kake, Oh Henry! and the Chicken Dinner, a chocolate peanut roll that actually survived until the 1960s.

The Three Musketeers bar was introduced in 1932 and has lasted ever since as one of America's most popular snacks. Today, it's a single bar, but the original Three Musketeers had 3 bars in one wrapper, each made to a different recipe.

Seven billion pounds of chocolate and sweets are manufactured each year in the United States.

Cheesecake is believed to have been invented in ancient Greece. It was served to the athletes during the first Olympic Games held in 776 BC.

The origins of ice cream can be traced back to the 4th century BC, when the Roman Emperor Nero sent servants up nearby mountains to collect ice, which was combined with fresh fruit and honey to make a cooling dessert.
In 6th-century China, cooks found a method of creating ice and milk mixtures, and ice cream was probably brought back from China by traders and introduced to Europe,

The first ice-cream parlour in America opened in New York City in 1776, and the treat became available to a much wider audience with the invention of refrigeration.

The "ice-cream sundae" was first created in 1881 by ice-cream shop-owner Ed Berners of Wisconsin, USA. Berners served his creation only on Sundays.

In 1904, Charles E. Menches of St Louis, USA, filled pastry cups with scoops of ice cream, thereby inventing the ice-cream cone. The take-away cone made its debut later that year at the St Louis World's Fair.

Over the centuries, the pizza was developed among the people of Naples, Italy. The modern pizza, with mozzarella cheese and tomato, was first made there by baker Raffaele Esposito in 1889, especially for the visit of Italian King Umberto I and Queen Margherita. This patriotic pizza of basil, tomato and mozzarella matched the new Italian flag's red, green and white, and became the Margherita, named after Her Majesty.

The little circular thing that keeps the pizza from hitting the inside of the box top is called a "package saver for pizza and cakes". It was invented by Carmela Vitale of New York, who filed for a US patent on February 10, 1983.

Clarence Birdseye invented a method for quick-freezing food in 1923. He sold the patents in 1929 for 22 million dollars.

The ancient Romans made toast. Tostum is the Latin word for scorching or burning.

The first electric toaster was invented in 1893 in the UK by Crompton and Co. It toasted one side of the bread at a time and it required a person to stand by and turn it off manually when the toast looked done. Charles Strite invented the modern pop-up toaster with a timer in 1919.

Thomas Adams tried to make chicle – a rubbery substance found in some trees – into car tyres and rain boots, without much success. One day, he absent-mindedly popped a piece of chicle into his mouth. Chewing away, he had the idea to add flavouring to the stuff. Shortly after, he opened the world's first chewing gum factory. In February 1871, Adams' New York Gum went on sale in shops for a penny a piece, and in 1888, an Adams' chewing gum called Tutti-Frutti became the first chewing gum to be sold in a vending machine.

In 1756, mayonnaise was invented in France by the chef of Duke de Richelieu. In 1905, the first ready-made mayonnaise was sold at Richard Hellman's New York delicatessen. In 1912, Richard's mayonnaise was mass marketed and sold under the name "Hellman's Blue Ribbon Mayonnaise".

Powdered milk was invented by ancient Mongolians, possibly as long as a thousand years ago. Italian traveller Marco Polo arrived in Mongolia in 1275 and stayed in Kublai Khan's court. Polo made written records of how the Mongols used powdered milk. They added millet and rice to milk, boiled it until thick, then let it dry.

A "Spork" is a cross between a spoon and a fork, sometimes called the "runcible spoon". A patent for the Spork was issued on August 11, 1970 to Van Brode Milling Company, of Massachusetts, USA.

WRONG, WRONG, WRONG!

Who Said Inventing was Easy?

Walter Hunt had no trouble thinking up new ideas. He invented a machine to spin cloth, a fire-engine gong, a forest saw, and a stove that burned hard coal. His inventions worked, but he never made any money from them. In 1849 he needed to pay a 15-dollar debt to a friend, so he came up with a new invention. From a piece of brass wire, coiled at the centre and shielded at one end, he made the first safety pin. He took out a patent on it, sold the rights for $400, paid his friend back and had $385 to spare. Then he watched his latest brainstorm go on to become a million- dollar money earner for someone else.

18th-century engineer Robert Fulton had to work hard to attract investors to build his new steamboat. The investors had one request; they asked that their names be kept secret in case people laughed at them for investing in a project that sounded so ridiculous.

Stock salesman Joshua Coppersmith was trying to sell stocks in a new telephone company in Boston, USA. He was arrested as a con-man for selling stocks in something that couldn't be done. People at the time thought it was impossible to send a voice over a wire.

In 1894, the President of the Royal Society in Britain, Lord Kelvin, predicted that radio had no future. The first radio factory opened five years later, and now there are over one billion radio sets in the world and more than 33,000 radio stations. He also predicted that heavier-than-air flying machines were impossible.

Mike Nesmith is a former member of the 1960s pop band the Monkees. His mother, Bette Nesmith Graham, was a creative individual herself. Her invention, liquid paper, was initially rejected by corporate giants IBM, so she set up her own cottage industry to make and sell it herself. She later sold the business for 47.5 million dollars.

With the advent of railways in the 19th century, one prominent American citizen proclaimed that they would create the need for dozens of new insane asylums to house all those who were driven mad by the noise and terrified by the size of the trains. The reputation of these new-fangled trains was no better in Europe. German experts predicted that if passenger trains travelled faster than 24 km/h (15 mph), the passengers would all get nosebleeds.

277

When Harry M. Warner, head of the Hollywood film studio Warner Brothers, was told about the possibility of movies with sound, he said, "Who the hell wants to hear actors talk?"

A Yale University management professor told one of his students, Fred Smith, that although his project idea was interesting, to earn better than a "C" grade, the idea had to be possible as well. Fred Smith's paper was a business proposal for a company offering a reliable overnight delivery service. He went on to found Federal Express.

When G. G. Hubbard learned of his future son-in-law's invention, he called it "only a toy". His daughter was engaged to a young man named Alexander Graham Bell, and the toy was the telephone.

"But what ... is it good for?" asked an engineer at the Advanced Computing Systems Division of IBM, in 1968, commenting on the microchip.

Even the inventor of the telephone, Alexander Graham Bell, didn't fully appreciate its future worldwide popularity, stating that it would be "useful for lonely farmers' wives".

"The wireless music box has no imaginable commercial value. Who would pay for a message sent to nobody in particular?" commented David Sarnoff's associates in response to his urgings for investment in radio in the 1920s.

Radio inventor Guiglelmo Marconi felt it might be a "useful replacement for Morse code wires".

Thomas Edison invented lots of things but he didn't invent the radio. In 1922 he declared that "the radio craze will die out in time."

When British merchant Peter Durand invented the metal can in 1810, he completely overlooked the need for a device to open it. The tin opener was invented some decades later.

When IBM conducted a market study of Chester Carlson's invention in 1959, the company concluded that it would take only 5,000 units of his new product to saturate the market. IBM therefore declined to be part of the new product introduction. Too bad for IBM. Carlson's invention was the photocopier, and his new product was the beginning of the Xerox Corporation. It is estimated that every day, worldwide, 3,000,000,000 photocopies are made.

In the early 20th century, a world market for only four million automobiles was forecast because it was thought the world would run out of chauffeurs.

Darryl F. Zanuck, of movie studios 20th Century Fox, thought television was just a passing fancy. In 1946, he said, "Television won't be able to hold any market after the first six months. People will soon get tired of staring at a plywood box every night."

Farmers rejected the first successful cast-iron plough in 1797. They believed the cast iron would poison the land and stimulate weeds, and in the mid-1800s, farmers tore down miles of new telegraph wire, fearful that the new fangled invention would disturb the weather and ruin crops.

Shortly after the end of World War Two in 1945, the whole of Volkswagen – the factory and all the patents – was offered, free, to Henry Ford, boss of the Ford Motor Company. He turned it down, dismissing the Volkswagen Beetle as a bad design. The Beetle became the best-selling vehicle of all time.

The telephone was not widely appreciated for the first 15 years of its existence because people did not see a use for it. In fact, in the British Parliament it was mentioned there was no need for telephones because "we have enough messengers here". Western Union, a US telegraph company, believed that it could never replace the telegraph. In 1876, an internal memo read: "This telephone has too many shortcomings to be seriously considered as a means of communication." Famous author, Mark Twain, upon being invited by Alexander Graham Bell to invest $5,000 in the new invention, could not see a future in the telephone, and turned him down.

"Computers in the future may weigh no more than 15 tons." – *Popular Mechanics* **magazine forecasting the relentless march of science in 1949.**

While still at college, Steve Jobs and Steve Wozniak took an invention they had been working on to Hewlett-Packard. They were told to come back when they'd left school. They didn't bother. The invention Hewlett-Packard turned down was the world's first personal computer. The two Steves went on to start their own company, Apple Computer Inc. The first Apple computer was born in Steve Jobs' parents' garage. Jobs and Wozniak worked furiously in that garage assembling computers for fellow students and were totally unprepared for their first commercial order for 50 computers. To raise the $1,300 needed for parts, Jobs sold his old Volkswagen camper van and Wozniak sold his Hewlett-Packard calculator. The next year, 1977, Apple sales reached $800,000. It was included on the Fortune 500 (a list of the largest US companies) in a record five years.

An eminent Irish scientist, Dr Dionysius Lardner (1793–1859) didn't believe that trains could contribute much in speedy transport. He wrote: "Travel at high speed is not possible, because passengers "would die of asphyxia [suffocation]". Today, trains reach speeds of 500 km/h (310 mph).

American physicist Robert Goddard's theory that rockets could operate in outer space met with a lot of criticism. Indeed, the New York Times printed an article ridiculing his ideas. The day after Apollo 11 left earth's orbit for the moon, largely due to Goddard's work, the newspaper published an apology.

But perhaps the guy who got it wrong most was the director of the United States Patent Office in 1899. He assured President William McKinley that "everything that can be invented has already been invented".

IT'LL NEVER WORK

Really Strange Inventions

12 Gauge Golf Club
US Patent 4,176,537

This golf club features a barrel, muzzle and a trap door in the back for loading an explosive charge. The firing pin is aligned so that when your club strikes the ball, it is literally blasted down the course!

Flying Fish
US patent 3,598,121

This angler's aid takes the sweat out of catching a big fish. A balloon floats on the water above your baited hook. When you feel a pull on your line, press the button on your fishing rod. The balloon fills with gas and your fish floats up out of the water!

Gravestone Sundial
French Patent 2780195

In this invention, a spike casts
a shadow on the gravestone.
At certain times of the year, the
shadow points to the deceased's
dates of birth, death and life events
carved onto the gravestone,
keeping passers-by informed of all
the anniversaries of the person's
life, even after their passing.

Junior Jail
US Patent 4,205,966

Changing a baby can be difficult when
the baby doesn't want to be changed.
But Junior Jail's "torso clamp" and
foot and arm restraints mean that
a baby can be practically bolted
to a table while its nappy
is changed.

Imaginary Pet Leash
International Patent WO9701384

This leash holds its shape as you walk and incorporates the lead and the collar in one. A tiny speaker in the collar is connected to switches in the leash handle, enabling the user to produce barks, growls and other appropriate pet noises on demand.

Snow Irrigator
UK Patent 1047735

This device pipes snow and ice balls from Antarctica to water the Australian desert, thereby solving the world food problem. The snowballs accelerate under gravity from 3,000 metres (10,000 feet) up on the Antarctic plateau, reaching speeds of up to 500 miles per hour, when they are shot through the pipelines thousands of miles long, using Earth's gravity and spinning energy to help them on their way,

Phone Gas
US Patent 5,308,063

This is an ingenious device for the parents of sick children who refuse to take their medicine. The medicine is contained in an inhaler in your telephone receiver. You call your child to the phone, which plays soothing music. Then at the push of a magic button, you gas him or her with the medicine, which comes squirting out of the mouthpiece!

Skin Stencil
US Patent 5,256,595

This is a cap designed with the sports fan in mind. It allows the cap wearer to actually burn his team's logo onto his forehead! The Skin Stencil has a cut-out design in the headband of the cap. The area around the cutout stencil blocks the sun from tanning your skin, while the logo will bronze onto your head!

Golf Practice Device
UK Patent 1251780

Light sensitive cells monitor the path of the club head as you swing it. If they detect that the player is about play a bad shot, and risk losing the ball in tall grass somewhere, a puff of compressed air passes along a pipe by the ball up into the middle of the tee. This blows the ball off the tee so that the player misses it completely, saving hours of ball-searching time.

Floating Furniture
US patent 4,888,836

This is a solution for people who live in small houses and have tables and chairs that are taking up too much space. This lighter-than-air inflatable furniture can be blown up with helium gas and stored on your ceiling when you're not using it! Need a nap? Just grab the tether rope and pull your bed off the ceiling! Also you can let the dining table float up to the ceiling after dinner, taking the dirty dishes out of your sight!

Dog Watch
US patent 5,023,850

A dog year is equal to seven human years, yes? Well then, every dog needs a watch that goes seven times faster than a normal one so he can tell the time too! The Dog Watch means Fido always knows how old he is, and he'll never be late for dinner!

Crunch Protector
US Patent 4,986,334

Everyone hates it when their breakfast cereal goes soggy. Well, you need suffer no longer with Crunch Protector! Simply fill the container under the milk bowl with sand to counter the weight of the cereal in the upper bowl. Now pour the cornflakes down the chute to the awaiting milk in the lower bowl and eat. Continue pouring and eating and pouring and eating. Each bite remains crunchy to the bottom of the bowl, ensuring breakfast satisfaction every time!

WHEEL SMART

Street Transport Takes Off

In-line skates were created back in the early 1700s when a Dutchman attached wooden spools to strips of wood and nailed them to his shoes. In 1980, two brothers from Minnesota, USA, Scott and Brennan Olsen, discovered an old in-line skate in a sports shop and thought the design would be perfect for off-season hockey training. They improved it and soon were manufacturing the first "Rollerblades" in their parents' basement. Hockey players and skiers soon caught on. Today 60 in-line skate manufacturers exist, but Rollerblades were the first with heel brakes and Active Brake Technology, and have over 200 other registered patents.

The skateboard started as a way of surfing on land. In the 1950s, Californian surfers, frustrated with bad weather, nailed the bases of roller skates to wooden planks. These boards allowed for "sidewalk surfing" down hills. The fad spread, and challenges were added, such as kerb-jumping. This became "street surfing". By the early 1970s, bike and toy companies were making boards with urethane wheels on flexible mounts. Riders' abilities improved along with the equipment. Skateboarding developed new moves, like the "Ollie", invented by Alan Ollie Gelf: it's a leap into the air during which the board stays flush with the feet. The empty swimming pools and building sites used for boarding were replaced by specially designed parks.

In 2003, skateboarding was America's sixth largest participant sport and, not content with the streets, the surfers are taking over the snow too!

SPARE PARTS

Invention Bits & Pieces

The inventor of the World Wide Web, British-born Tim Berners-Lee, never made any money from his invention, which completely changed the computer world. In 1989 he came up with a way to link documents on the Internet using hypertext, so "surfers" could jump from one document to another through highlighted words. He decided not to patent his technology since he feared that, if he did patent it, use of the Web would be too expensive and would therefore not become used worldwide. He passed up a certain fortune so that the world could learn and communicate.

Coca-Cola was originally green.

In the early 1970s, Hungarian architect Erno Rubik designed geometric models in his spare time and came up with a cube, with each face consisting of nine smaller cubes. He used it to teach algebraic group theory, but a Hungarian trading company saw its potential as a toy and began marketing it. By 1980, more than 100 million Rubik's Cubes had been sold around the world, as well as another 50 million "knock-off" cubes produced illegally by rival toymakers. More than 50 books were published explaining how to solve the puzzle.

The computer was launched in 1943, more than 100 years after Charles Babbage designed the first one. Babbage dropped his idea after he couldn't raise money for it. In 1998, the Science Museum in London built a working replica of Babbage's machine, using the materials available at Babbage's time. It worked just as Babbage had intended.

The yo-yo may be the second oldest toy in the world after the doll. There are ancient Greek yo-yos in museums in Athens and yo-yos are pictured on the walls of Egyptian temples. Carving and playing with yoyos is a traditional pastime in the Philippines, but when Phillipino Pedro Flores moved to the USA in the 1920s and worked as a bellhop at a Santa Monica hotel, he found his lunchtime hobby was drawing a crowd! He started a company to make the toys, and sold it, together with the name "Yoyo" in 1929 to Donald F. Duncan. Duncan introduced the looped slip-string (which allows for advanced tricks), the first plastic yo-yos and the Butterfly-shaped yo-yo. Donald Duncan made a fortune, but lost it all again when the 1950s fad ended, largely through fighting costly court cases trying to stop competitors from making their own versions.

In 1879, Auguste Bartholdi received a design patent for the Statue of Liberty.

Eight-year-old Theresa Thompson and her nine-year-old sister, Mary, received a US patent in 1960. They had invented a solar-heated tent, which they called a "Wigwarm".

Six-year-old Suzanna Goodin, tired of cleaning the cat food spoon, invented an edible spoon-shaped cracker for pets. She won a grand prize for her idea in a National Invention Contest.

Melting ice cream inspired the invention of the outboard motor. Ole Evinrude was rowing his boat to his local island picnic spot and, as he rowed, his ice cream melted in the sun. Ole started thinking about making the trip quicker so he could enjoy his picnic unmelted. He invented the outboard motor, a handy device for any boater worried about their dessert.

The formulas for Cola-Cola and Silly Putty have never been patented. These trade secrets are shared with only a few company employees. There have been many attempts to duplicate the products, but so far, none has been successful.

Bar codes were invented by Bernard Silver and Norman Woodland in 1948, but it was over twenty years before the first bar-coded item was sold. It was a pack of Wrigley's chewing gum in 1974.

More than a million people got Pet Rocks for Christmas in 1975. Gary Dahl, of Los Gatos, California, was joking with friends about his easy-to-care-for pet, a rock! It ate nothing and didn't bark or chew the furniture. The Pet Rock was sold with a funny manual that included tips on how to teach it tricks. By 1976, Gary was a millionaire many times over.

Arthur Melin and Richard Knerr, founders of the Wham-O toy company, took an idea from Australia, where students exercised using bamboo hoops, and turned it into the biggest fad of all time. The Hula Hoop is a round plastic tube that can be rotated around the waist by swinging the hips. It can also be jumped through, skipped over, or spun around the neck. Four months after the launch, Wham-O had sold over twenty million of them.

A huge fad in the mid 1970s, Mood Rings were made of heat-sensitive liquid crystals encased in quartz. When the body temperature of the wearer changed, the crystals changed colour, supposedly indicating the wearer's mood. Blue meant happy; red meant insecure; green meant active; black meant tense. Joshua Reynolds, a 33-year-old New Yorker, was the creative genius behind them.

Long before starring in *Toy Story*, Mr Potato Head was the first ever toy to be advertised on TV. In 1985, he received four write-in votes in the election for Mayor of Boise, Idaho, USA.

In the year 2000, Jacob Dunnack forgot to bring his baseball when he brought his bat to his grandma's house. Needless to say, he was disappointed, but he came up with an ingenious way of making sure it didn't happen again. The JD Batball is a plastic baseball bat with a removable cap so the balls can be stored inside and won't get lost. This handy invention means kids can carry their bat and balls with one hand, while never worrying about forgetting or losing their baseballs again. Jacob Dunnack invented it when he was six years old.

To encourage use of his new invention, the shopping cart, market owner Sylvan Goldman hired fake shoppers to push the carts around his store in Oklahoma City, USA. He had to do this because the real customers didn't want to touch his invention.

Early Egyptian, Chinese, Greek and Roman writings describe numerous mixtures for toothpaste. The more palatable ingredients included powdered fruit, burnt shells, talc, honey and dried flowers. The less appetizing ones included mice and lizard livers.

The first commercial vacuum cleaner was so large it was mounted on a wagon. People threw parties in their homes so that guests could watch the new device do its job.

Becky Schroeder began her patenting career when she was just 14 years old. She put luminous paint on a piece of paper, and put it under her writing paper so that she could write in the dark. This invention has been used in all sorts of ways. Doctors use it in hospitals to read patients' charts at night without waking them, and astronauts use it when their electrical systems are turned down for recharging.

The first ballpoint pen was invented by Hungarian journalist Laslo Biro and his chemist brother, Georg, in 1938.

At just nine years old, in the 1850s, Margaret Knight began working in a cotton mill, where she saw a steel-tipped shuttle fly out of a loom and hit a nearby worker. As a result, Margaret devised her first invention: a shuttle restraining device. She went on to invent the machine that makes the square-bottomed paper bags still used for groceries in America.

Several people are credited with the invention of the flush toilet. Most famously, the hilariously named Thomas Crapper was the sanitary engineer who invented the valve-and-siphon arrangement that made the modern toilet possible. Another claimant to "the throne" was British inventor Alexander Cumming,

who patented a toilet in 1775. However, archeologists have discovered on the island of Crete the remains of what looks like a flush toilet that is believed to be 4,000 years old.

Galileo invented the thermometer in 1593.

Bullet-proof vests, fire escapes, windshield wipers and laser printers were all invented by women.

Robert Adler has the dubious distinction of being the father of the couch potato. Back in 1955, Adler was employed by what was then Zenith Radio Corporation, where he was asked to invent something that would allow viewers to turn down the TV volume without leaving their chairs. Early versions were attached to the set by a wire, which people could fall over. Then Adler hit on the idea of using sound waves, and the remote control was born.

As a health precaution, Alexander Graham Bell covered the windows in his home to block out what he thought were the harmful rays of the full moon!

The first rickshaw was invented in 1869 by an American Baptist minister, the Reverend E. Jonathan Scobie, to transport his invalid wife around the streets of Yokohama in Japan.

Melville Stone was a self-made man, who worked his way up from newspaper delivery boy to publisher of the *Chicago Daily News*. When Stone first started his newspaper in 1875, the price of a copy was one cent. Circulation rose rapidly at first, then levelled off. Then sales started to drop. When Stone investigated why fewer people were buying his paper, he discovered the problem had nothing to do with its quality, but largely that one-cent coins were in short supply, and

nobody wanted to break a dollar for the sake of a one-cent newspaper. Stone decided he had to do something. First he visited the United States mint in Philadelphia and organised the shipment of barrels of one-cent coins to Chicago. His problem then became how to get the coins into circulation quickly. So Stone persuaded Chicago merchants to sponsor "odd-price sales", during which they would sell their merchandise for a cent under the regular price: $8.99, $10.99, $12.99 and so on. The odd prices did the trick. People had cent coins to get rid of again, and sales of the *Chicago Daily News* flourished once more.

In addition to the successful injection of the coins into the Chicago area, Stone had invented a phenomenon. The traders found that the penny off had a psychological effect on customers, making products seem cheaper ... and that's why so many prices today end in 99 (cents, for example).

FROM FOOT TO FERRARI

A Brief History of Driving

10,000 BC Nobody driving, anywhere.

6500 BC Wheel invented by Sumerians.

3500 BC Sumerians have animal-drawn vehicles.

500 BC First roads built by Persians.

1690 Early bicycle invented in France.

1765 Steam engine invented in the UK.

1824 Internal combustion engine first theorised by Sadi Carnot, France.

1868 First traffic signal, invented in the UK.

1884 Motorcycle invented in the UK.

1885 Car with internal combustion engine designed by Karl Benz, Germany.

1891 Front-engined car designed in France.

1908 Cars mass produced in the US.

1929 Ferrari founded, Enzo Ferrari, Italy.

FROM HUMBLE BEGINNINGS

Start Small - Get Big!

As a child, legendary physicist Albert Einstein was expelled from his school.

Chester Greenwood was born in Maine, USA, in 1858. A school dropout, he spent a lot of time ice skating, where his ears suffered from the cold. Making two loops from wire, he asked his grandmother to sew fur around them. Greenwood's Champion Ear Protectors were born and became famous. Chester made a substantial fortune supplying his Ear Protectors to, among others, the US Army. And in 1977, the state of Maine declared December 21 "Chester Greenwood Day!"

One morning in 1903, Albert J. Parkhouse arrived as usual at his workplace, the Timberlake Wire and Novelty Company in Michigan, USA, which specialised in making lampshade frames and other wire items. When he went to hang his hat and coat on the hooks provided for the workers, Parkhouse found they were all in use. Albert picked up a piece of wire, bent it into two large oblong hoops opposite each other, and twisted both ends at the centre into a hook. Then he hung up his coat and went to work.

The company apparently thought the "coat-hanger" was a good idea, because they took out a patent on it. In those days, companies were allowed to take out patents on any of their employees' inventions. The company made a fortune, and Albert never got a penny.

The discoverer of gravity, Isaac Newton, was thought to be a slow learner at school.

When Henry Ford started his production line car factory in the US, he was widely celebrated as a great innovator and copied throughout the world. His line wasn't such a hit with his workers, however. They complained that they were slaves to the machines and nine out of ten of the employees Ford hired walked out when they discovered their working conditions.

Nolan Bushnell spent more time running the games at a local amusement park than he did on his studies at the University of Utah, USA. In fact, he graduated at the bottom of his engineering class. His dreams of working for Disney's amusement empire were dashed – the company wouldn't hire him. Nolan day-dreamed about electronic versions of popular games. He invented Pong, the first video game, and went on to found the Atari video games company.

In 1850, the California gold rush was in full swing and everyday items were in short supply. Levi Strauss, a 20-year-old Bavarian immigrant, left New York for San Francisco with a small supply of rough canvas to sell for use as tents and wagon covers.

A prospector convinced Levi to make him some hardwearing work trousers from the canvas. They were a success, and other prospectors bought work trousers from Levi. Looking to improve on his design, Levi came across Serge de Nimes, a twill cloth from France that was hardy yet more comfortable to wear than his canvas. This cloth was to become known as "denim", and Levi's jeans were to become the most famous item of clothing on Earth. And they still are.

Orville Wright's first flight, which was largely responsible for the birth of the aviation industry, lasted a mere twelve seconds.

In 1886, Atlanta pharmacist John S. Pemberton invented a medicinal mixture for people who were tired, nervous or suffering from toothache. He took some of his new "health syrup" to a local shop. Instead of being mixed with ice water, as he had instructed, the syrup was mixed with soda water, making it fizzy. But Pemberton liked the taste and decide to market his health brew as a refreshing drink instead.

Pemberton's bookkeeper drew a fancy logo for the new product. The name they decided on was a mix of two of the ingredients, the coca leaf and the kola nut. It wasn't an immediate success – Mr Pemberton sold just fifty dollars' worth of "Coca-Cola" in his first year – but sales improved, and how! Today the world drinks one billion Coca-Cola Company products every single day.

Henry Ford, the man who brought cheap cars to the masses, also invented the barbecue-friendly charcoal briquette in 1920.

In 1933, Charles B. Darrow played a game he'd drawn on the cloth on his kitchen table – an exciting battle over property and fortune. He played at home with his family and friends, who found it addictive and asked for sets of their own. Charles went to work, making hand-made copies and selling them at four dollars each. Demand for the game grew beyond his ability to fill orders, and he took it to game company Parker Brothers, who rejected it. Undaunted, Charles continued to produce his hand-made editions and was highly successful. Finally Parker Brothers came to their senses and decided to buy the rights. The American people took to it in their millions. In 1935, under the Parker Brothers label, "Monopoly" became America's best-selling game. Darrow became a millionaire many times over, and today an estimated 500 million people worldwide play along.

Thomas Edison showed an inquisitive spirit at the tender age of six. He set the family barn on fire "just to see what it would do" and he tried to make a friend fly by feeding him a gas-producing laxative.

Earl Dickson's wife was rather accident prone, so he set out to develop a bandage that she could apply without help. He placed a small piece of gauze in the centre of a small piece of surgical tape, and what we know today as sticking plasters were born.

Joseph Priestly, the man who discovered oxygen, never took a science course.

In a vote for "Toy of the 20th Century", the winner was Lego. Game of the Century was Monopoly and Craze of the Century was the Yo-yo. Shortlisted entries included Action Man, Barbie, the teddy bear, Meccano, Scrabble, Mastermind and Trivial Pursuit.

Russian immigrant Conrad Hubert travelled to the US in 1890. He worked in a cigar store and a restaurant for a while, and he tried repairing watches. He was always broke. Conrad met a friend named Joshua Cowen who had invented a plant pot with a battery in it. Electricity from the battery made the flower in the pot light up when a button was pressed. Conrad decided he would try to sell these electric flower pots. Presently, Joshua became interested in something new and he sold his friend the flower pot idea for almost nothing. Conrad had an idea for a modification. He took the battery, the bulb and a paper tube and remade it into what he called "an electric hand torch." Hubert sold his invention as a novelty, but the usefulness of the torch soon became clear. When he died in 1928, Hubert was worth eight million dollars, which in 1928 was an awful lot of cash.

In 1907, James Murray Spangler, a janitor in Ohio, USA, deduced that the carpet sweeper he used was giving him a cough. He attached an old fan motor to his broom handle, using a pillow case as a dust collector. Spangler had invented an electric vacuum cleaner. He patented it in 1908, and formed the Electric Suction Sweeper Company. One of the first buyers was a cousin, whose husband, William H. Hoover, president of the Hoover Company, gave James a job. Before long there was a Hoover vacuum cleaner in homes everywhere.

In 1888, Marvin Stone made the first paper drinking straws. Before his straws, beverage drinkers used natural rye grass. Stone made his prototype straw by winding a strip of paper around a pencil and sticking it together. He decided the ideal straw was 22 centimetres (eight and a half inches) long with a diameter just narrow enough to stop a lemon pip.

CELEBRITY INVENTORS

More than One String to Their Bows

American War of Independence hero, Paul Revere, invented a process for cold rolling copper. The unpatented process was used to make plates for the boilers of early steamships.

Abraham Lincoln, congressman from Illinois, received a patent for "A Device for Buoying Vessels over Shoals". The idea of the invention was that if a ship ran aground in shallow waters, the bellows would be filled with air, and the ship would float clear. Lincoln became US President, and the model he whittled for his boat floater invention can be seen at the Smithsonian National Museum in Washington.

Edie Adams, singer and comedienne, patented a cigar holder-ring which she used in TV ads for Muriel cigars in the 1960s. It was designed to show women that it was ladylike to smoke cigars.

Danny Kaye, comedian and movie star, patented a "blow-out" party toy. Unlike the traditional "blow-out" toy that unfurls straight out, Kaye's unfurled in three directions at once.

American Statesman Benjamin Franklin invented bifocals because he hated having to wear two pairs of glasses.

Movie star Jamie Lee Curtis patented a nappy that ingeniously incorporates a handy pocket to hold moistened towelettes, so that the mucky baby and the means to clean it are always in the same place.

Rudyard Kipling, author of *The Jungle Book*, lived in Vermont, America in the 1890s. One chilly winter, he invented the game of snow golf. He painted his golf balls red so that they could be located in the white stuff.

A patent was issued in 1970 to movie legend Steve McQueen – a by-product of his racing cars hobby was the invention of a bucket seat.

Tom Sawyer author Mark Twain received a patent for "An Improvement in Adjustable and Detachable Straps for Garments". He later received two more patents: one for a self-pasting scrapbook and one for a game to help players remember important historical dates.

TV diver Jacques Cousteau co-invented the aqualung, allowing divers to stay in the depths of the sea for extended periods.

The first rubber balloons were made by English physicist and electrical pioneer, Michael Faraday, in 1824, for use in his experiments with hydrogen at the Royal Institution in London. Toy balloons were introduced by rubber maker Thomas Hancock the following year in the form of a kit consisting of a bottle of rubber solution and a syringe. Faraday went on to star on the £20 note for his scientific achievements, but didn't make a fortune from his balloons.

Hedy Lamarr, an Austrian movie actress, invented a radio guiding system for torpedoes which was used in World War Two. She gained the knowledge from her first husband, Fritz Mandl, a Viennese arms dealer who sided with the Nazis. Hedy drugged her maid to escape her husband and homeland, fled to America and became a Hollywood star.

Harry Houdini, the magician, received a patent for a "Diver's Suit" enabling the wearer to "quickly divest himself of the suit while being submerged and to safely escape and reach the surface of the water".

MR THUNDER & LIGHTNING

Nikola Tesla

Inventor and engineer Nikola Tesla was born in Croatia in 1856.

He first went to the US in 1884 to work for Thomas Edison, who had problems with his Direct Current system of electricity. He promised Tesla rich rewards if he could fix it. Tesla ended up saving Edison a fortune, but Edison went back on his agreement. Tesla resigned, and devised a better system for electrical transmission – the Alternating Current system we use in our homes today. He then invented the motors that are used in all household appliances. He was using fluorescent bulbs in his lab forty years before industry "invented" them.

At the World's Fair in 1893 in Chicago, he made glass tubes in the shapes of famous scientists' names – the first neon signs. He designed the world's first hydro-electric plant, located in Niagara Falls, and patented the first speedometer for cars.

The jealous Edison did his best to discredit Tesla at every turn, declaring that AC electricity was dangerous. So at the 1893 World Fair, Tesla demonstrated how safe AC was by passing it through his body to power light bulbs. He then shot lightning bolts to the crowd without harm. In 1898, he exhibited the first remote controlled model boat at Madison Square Garden, and he demonstrated the principles behind radio nearly ten years before Marconi. In 1943, the US Supreme Court ruled that Marconi's patents were invalid due to Tesla's previous work. Yet still he is not widely credited with the invention of radio.
But Tesla had his dark side too ...

He got a steam-driven oscillator to vibrate at the same frequency as the ground, creating an earthquake several miles in area. He stated that this technology could be used to split the Earth in half!

During World War One, the US government sought a way to detect German submarines, and put Edison in charge. Tesla proposed the use of energy waves – what we know today as radar – but Edison rejected Tesla's idea, and the world had to wait another 25 years for its invention.

Tesla died poor, aged 86, in 1943. In his lifetime, he received over 800 patents. Scientists continue to scour his notes, and many of his theories are just now being proven. Tesla might just be the greatest scientist who ever lived. If it wasn't for a jealous Thomas Edison, he would be a household name today.

The Big Book of MONSTERS!

Dare you read the scariest book around?

The Big Book of Monsters is packed with jokes,
facts, stories and games about all sorts of monsters.
You'd better check under your bed tonight . . .

ISBN: 0 603 56150 0